PSYCHIC & UFO REVELATIONS IN THE LAST DAYS

PSYCHIC &
UFO REVELATIONS
IN THE
LAST DAYS

Timothy Green Beckley

INNER LIGHT PUBLICATIONS

Published by:
INNER LIGHT PUBLICATIONS
P.O. BOX 753
NEW BRUNSWICK, N.J. 08903
Current book catalog sent free upon request.

CONTENTS

CHAPTER ONE

The End Times Are They Upon Us?

Since the first edition of this book was released almost 10 years ago many have written to say that I somehow changed their lives, because besides the somewhat dreary forecasts of doom and gloom, I managed to give a glimpse of a better world brought about by changes from the very core of humankind's cosmic heart. And while society has been in a constant flux, we still have a long ways to go before all the damage can be repaired.

It is unfortunate, but many of us get up every morning expecting that we will never see another sunset. With the world situation the way it is — and promises to be! — I don't think many of us would be too surprised to find out that some world leader had finally pushed the panic button that means the start of World War III. By writing this book, I don't mean to frighten the reader, but I do think you have the right to be prepared for what might happen in the very near — the immediate! — future. There is one thing that scientists, scholars, Biblical students, psychics and UFO contactees all seem to agree on, and that is that our planet is slated to undergo many changes. They may all see it happening in a slightly different way, but they agree one hundred percent that the End Times could be pretty close.

THE SITUATION KEEPS GETTING WORSE

Everyday the situation seems to get worse. Turn on the television, pick up a paper or read a news magazine and its obvious that the very fiber of society is breaking down around us.

Our civilization seems to be facing problems in many different areas — all of which could be of devastating consequences.

Crime in our inner cities is out of control. Purse and jewelry snatchers ride the mass transit systems looking for victims. People are pushed in front of subway trains. Gangs of youths threaten bus riders. Muggings take

With more countries entering the nuclear race chances of another world war increase each day.

place every few minutes. Hard drugs are sold openly in the street. It is unsafe in many communities to go out at night. Elderly people are repeated victims of break-ins and robberies. Gun-toting madmen stalk the streets mortally wounding innocent bystanders. All around us authority is being challenged, and authority appears powerless to do anything about the situation.

On the international scene, war and rumors of war appear on the horizon. Governments battle each other endlessly over political and religious ideals, as well as for that valuable substance known as oil. World War III could start any minute, as any number of nations now have the capability to build nuclear weapons.

In Iran and other parts of the globe, the United States is accused of Imperialism and told not to meddle in the internal affairs of other nations. We are told to keep out, *or else!* The tension is mounting in both the East and the West. Headlines talk openly about who may push the panic button first and send missiles flying to distant targets. Both sides think they are right and won't budge an inch. They appear determined to have their way, and the people be damned. And how could we forget the always tense situation between Israel and the Arab nations? They have long been at war, but now with the advent of nuclear weapons, they could easily drag the rest of the world into the battle.

Ecologically the Earth is in a state of turmoil. Everyday we hear about a new natural disaster of some sort. The planet we live on seems to be reeling back and forth, as if it is trying to rid itself of all the manmade problems we are forcing upon this once green planet. One is made to think twice about all the earthquakes, volcanic eruptions, tidal waves, freak storms, changing weather, and all the strange things that continue to happen around us. It becomes apparent that there is just cause for Mother Nature to "freak out" and turn against us. Calm thinking is necessary, but can all these catastrophies be coincidental? You and I would be utter fools to believe so.

TIME IS TICKING AWAY

Ask the man in the street and the vast majority will tell you they are convinced time is ticking away. And while "prophets of doom" have existed in other eras, there has never been such unanimous agreement as to the state of affairs we find ourselves in.

Many psychics and sensitives are leaving metropolitan areas and are telling their friends to "get out" before it is too late. They feel that the large cities will not be "safe" places to reside should our problems continue to mount.

There is a definite stillness in the air which indicates to anyone whose "third eye" is open, that things are not as they should be. The "vibes," if you care to call them that, are certainly not all that good. I for one have noticed lately that people are starting to talk of survival if the worse does come. They don't seem exactly sure of the way it will arrive. It could, they feel be a war, a global disaster, or some sort of BIG change in their own life that will uproot them in the middle of what they are doing.

As a researcher who has always been interested in expanding my knowledge of prophecy, UFO contacts, and psychic matters in general, I have recently found myself collecting a vast assortment of material from various sources, pertaining to the changing time in which we find ourselves thrown. I seem mysteriously drawn to this project. Over the years, I have established many personal friendships with New Age leaders. These contacts have proven very valuable in my obtaining bits and pieces of important research data. This data has led me to believe the earth could soon be going through what I call a DOOMSDAY PHASE.

While all this may sound very negative, there is a positive side to my findings, for we are being told by a "highly intelligent authority" what can be done to save our necks. Some of us, it seems, will actually be removed from this troubled planet before the end arrives. Also, it is not impossible to alter our misguided ways and change the outlook from bad to good. But in any regard, reading this book *word for word* could possibly save you great pain, worry, and discomfort in what may be just down the road.

CHAPTER TWO

Looking To The Stars For Salvation

Even the most skeptical of persons would find it difficult to admit that strange things haven't been seen in the sky. Of course, there is considerable dispute about just what has been observed. The scientific approach seems to be something like this: "I'll hide my head in the sand and it will go away." But the truth of the matter is that flying saucers have been around a long time. Biblical and historical references suggest they have been "watching over" us for centuries (perhaps since the beginning of time). In recent years, they showed up in ever-increasing numbers following World War II and the explosion of the first Atomic bomb.

Every day there are at least two new reports from somewhere in the world. During peak sighting periods that figure is increased by leaps and bounds. UFOs have been picked up on radar. They have been chased by our fastest military planes. They have landed many, many times, and have left behind physical evidence in the form of burned patches of earth, and indentations in the soil, as well as strange artifacts, like nothing to be found elsewhere on our planet.

What is not so widely known is that hundreds of ordinary people like you and I have actually come face-to-face with the aliens who operate these futuristic craft. And while a variety of space beings have been seen, the vast majority of humanoids who have been encountered look remarkably human. In fact, there are even those who say that aliens have arrived on this planet and are living amongst us.

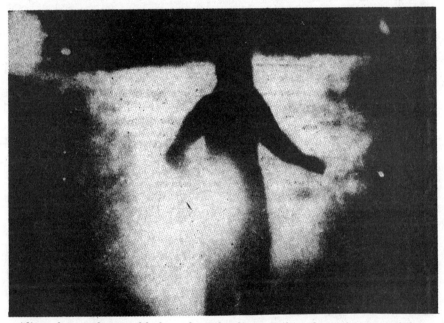

Aliens from other worlds have been landing on this planet for several decades in craft which we call UFOs or flying saucers. Some people have even made contact with these beings and say they are here to help us in our present situation.

In recent years — since 1950 or there abouts — a small segment of the population who refer to themselves as "contactees" have come forward and claimed to be in some sort of communication with the

UFOnauts, on a regular basis. In most cases no verbal words are spoken. Instead, there appears to be a transference of thought. A sort of mind-to-mind contact where the exchange of ideas is done via ESP or mental telepathy. It would appear from these cases that we are dealing with a superior intelligence; a race of beings who are thousands of years beyond our present state of development. In almost all of these contact stories a feeling of peace, love and warmth is felt radiating from these interplanetary beings. They tell us that they are coming here to assist humankind through these troubled times. They bring with them a general warning to humankind to mend its ways. They say that they themselves have gone through similar periods and survived because they learned how to live in harmony with the Universe as well as their fellow beings. They are offering their hand in help if we will listen and heed their words. However, they have informed all those who are willing to listen that they are powerless to prevent the worst from taking place if we refuse to acknowledge their existence — something which world leaders and the military have refused to do.

The themes that they keep harping on are those we have already mentioned, mainly world tension, ecological decay and the collapse of society. The following cases taken from the files of the UFO REVIEW, a publication I have published for many years, amply illustrates this point.

CASE ONE — JOHNNY SANDS, JANUARY 29th, 1976, LAS VEGAS, NEVADA

"I was 14 or 15 miles outside of Vegas, heading Southwest on the Blue Diamond Highway," states Country-Western singer, Johnny Sands, who had been performing that evening in a well known Las Vegas hotel. "I was headed back into town when I noticed a light to the side of me coming along the same way I was driving. It was quite high up, but it was losing altitude." Sands' car malfunctioned and he thought he was running short of fuel. "I pulled over to the side of the road and got out of the automobile. I opened the gas cap and shook the rear of the car to see if the gas would flush. I could hear gas so I went around to the front of the car and raised the hood. As I pushed the hood upward over my head I noticed there was a craft directly over me, about a thousand feet in the sky."

The musician says the craft landed and two beings emerged from the object. One of the UFOnauts proceeded to walk toward Sands until he stood right in front of him. "The being looked to be about 5 feet 8 inches tall and was completely bald. His face was really pale. He had no eyebrows, no eyelashes — no hair at all. To me he looked like somebody frozen to death."

The alien and the singer communicated by telepathy. "He touched something on his belt and right after he did so I got impressions in my mind. It was like listening to someone talking over the telephone from a great distance away." The being asked what the lights were in the distance and what Sands was doing in the desert.

At one point during their conversation the alien placed his hands behind his back and brought them back out in front of him seconds later. "In his hands," notes Sands, "he held a silver ball the approximate size of a basketball. He held it out in front of him as he turned back to me. He let the ball go and it floated there right in front of us. He passed his hands over the object and made it start rotating in a circular motion as the earth rotates around the sun. He started to explain something that tied in with our nuclear devices, and why they were coming here. He said nuclear devices cause a 'confliction' in the galaxy — those were his exact words. He then put his hand over the top of the ball, and as he did so there was an explosion just above its smooth surface. There was a flash, a minor explosion like a firecracker going off and an eruption similar to a volcano. Next, the ball started to act up a bit, as if it were being stirred up by the explosion. He said that when we use nuclear devices that it causes both our world as well as his planet to vibrate like this. He added that because of these tremors, the rotation of the Earth is slowing down, and we are actually losing time, and thus we grow older much faster." Sands admits that the alien did not go into detail nor did he explain any of the things which he said. However, the performer contends that all during the conversation he felt like he was talking to a very wise person, who had been around a long time.

CASE TWO — HELIO AGUIAR, APRIL 24th, 1959
BRAZILIAN COAST

Senor Helio Aguiar was riding a motorcycle along the Brazilian coast near Amaralian when he happened to see a "black spot" out over the Atlantic Ocean. As the object came closer it resembled a large silvery disc. There were windows on the craft and a number of strange markings on the underbelly of the UFO. In front of the witness the object played "looping the loop" in the sky. As the UFO approached, Senor Aguiar's motorcycle stalled and he felt a strong pressure on his head. For a brief period of time the witness lost consciousness. when he came to he found clutched in his hand a piece of paper upon which he had apparently written a message while he was unconscious. The message was short and quite simple. It read: *"Put an absolute stop to all atomic tests for war-like purposes. The balance of the Universe is threatened. We shall remain vigilant and ready to intervene."*

CASE THREE — STUART WHITMAN, NOVEMBER, 1965,
NEW YORK CITY

Stuart Whitman is not just another UFO witness. He also just happens to be one of Hollywood's most talented actors, who is probably best known for his appearance in the award-winning motion picture, The Sound and the Fury. Whitman's soul searching experience occurred on the night of the famous blackout when lights went out up and down the east coast.

The veteran performer had just that afternoon checked in at a mid-town Manhattan hotel. He had gone to bed reasonably early when around one in the morning a high-pitched buzzing sound began to fill the room arousing him from his slumber. From out of the dark recesses of the room, he heard his name being called repeatedly. "WHITMAN — WHITMAN, do you hear us?" Lifting himself onto his elbows the dedicated actor scanned his immediate surroundings in an effort to detect who was calling out his name. "My first impression was that someone from the hotel had unlocked my door with a master key and was trying to attract my attention." The only source of light around him seemed to be coming from outside his hotel room. "I parted the curtains and looked out onto a city thrown into total darkness. I had gone to bed earlier because I realized there was no place to go and nothing to do. The great metropolis that is New York had come to a total standstill."

As he stood by the window which looked out over Central Park, Whitman saw "two brightly lit orange-colored eggs," that were hovering in a haze not more than a hundred yards away from him.

As he watched he heard the mysterious "voice" speak once again. "They told me that they — the intelligence behind UFOs — were responsible for the blackout. They said they had taken this action to prove to the people of the world that they are real and capable of phenomenal undertakings. The reason for their being involved in such an 'experiment' they said, was obvious. They told me they are worried over our continued testing and development of nuclear weapons. This to them was a peaceful 'show of force'. In addition, they are apparently concerned about the chaos of society and the decay of our world governments. They said the blackout was only a small demonstration of the power they possess to stop us from annihilating our civilization and nearby planets. They said in so many words that they will interfere if we go too far in our war-like attitudes. They claimed that they are able to stop all electrical apparatus from functioning, and could put a halt to our normal activities any time they wanted to!"

Stuart Whitman's strange experience was written up in several papers at the time, but was soon forgotten. However, several years after the blackout along with fellow researcher, Harold Salkin, I interviewed the actor on the telephone and managed to get additional details that were not known at the time.

CASE FOUR — GERMANA GROSSO — ITALY

This account is from a woman in Italy who also says space aliens are very benevolent. After a life long relationship with these beings, Germana Grosso broke her silence and spoke to a newspaper in Turin.

Beings from outer space have set up bases on Earth beneath the Gobi Desert and even in Italy, according to the quiet 53 year old spinster, who lives with her mother.

Miss Grosso said she has been in touch with them for 20 years and they told her: "Our main enemy on earth is the complete lack of mutual love and understanding amongst humans." She said she has been chosen by them to issue an urgent appeal "choose love, not war."

On July 10 several years ago, spacemen told her "there will be an immense catastrophe for earthmen when a terrible earthquake will claim many victims." Shortly afterwards, China and the Philippines were struck by earthquakes.

On May 19, Miss Grosso was told "a volcano is going to erupt with tremendous violence." She is certain that this meant La Soufriere Volcano on the island of Guadaloupe.

Miss Grosso is respected by all her neighbors. She is calm and thoughtful and in no way hysterical or excitable.

How did she start contacting spacemen, resulting in several thousand typed pages of telepathic messages from them?

"I started 20 years ago through a Tibetan Lama who contacted me by telepathy," she said. "He explained that I could converse with beings from outer space."

Soon she was speaking to them and seeing them as though on a television screen. She has painted over 70 pictures of spacemen with long ascetic faces, large eyes and long hair as well as female dragonflies floating about in an ethereal world.

There are also Egyptian scenes from the times of the Pharoahs all in microscopic detail.

Although Miss Grosso has no scientific education, many of her typed space messages contain highly technical terms.

Miss Grosso said that these beings from outer space were named "Back" living on a planet called Lioaki.

They have numerous bases on Earth already, Miss Grosso maintained, with one under the Gobi Desert and another under Sousa Valley, northern Italy. She said this base accounted for the number of flying saucers seen in this region in the past.

The "Back" spacemen also had a base deep under the Atlantic Ocean and this accounted for the series of mystery sea and air tragedies in the so-called "Bermuda Triangle" as ships and planes tangled with arriving or departing spaceships.

Miss Grosso said she had broken her silence at the urging of the spacemen to launch an urgent appeal for world brotherhood to save Earth from disaster. "The spacemen are only interested in giving us a warning, and do not want to interfere with human history or Earth's destiny," she added.

Such cases similar to those we have detailed above literally abound in UFO literature. However, many of the civilian UFO research groups refuse to give credit to such stories, wishing to believe reports of lights in the sky, but rejecting all alien philosophy that might come through during any close encounter. Other reports like these include the story of a Soviet woman parachutist who said that she had been "captured" in mid-air and "given a message for the authorities," which told them to disarm their nuclear warheads, as well as the more recent case of sergeant Charles L. Moody who was abducted on board a UFO while in the Arizona desert. According to Moody, beings visiting Earth from several other planets "fear for their own lives" because of what is happening on our planet. He says their mission is a peaceful one, but they they will "protect themselves at all costs."

AN ECOLOGICAL MISSION

Following the repeated appearance of UFOs and alien beings in New Jersey, Chicago parapsychologist Warren Frieberg flew into Newark Airport with his wife to try and make contact with the space intelligence responsible for these sightings.

The press gathered on the roof of the Stonehenge apartment building in North Bergen, to witness a unusual — but not altogether unique — experiment. A psychic researcher and professional hypnotist, Frieberg was about to place Libby, a trained trance channel in an altered state of consciousness. While in a relaxed and receptive state of mind, it was hoped that she would be able to establish telepathic contact with the occupants of a flying saucer that had landed in North Hudson Park (located directly across from the ultra-modern high rise), and had been observed several times collecting soil samples in the dead of night.

Up some thirty floors above the street and only a stones'-throw away from the Hudson River, a harsh north wind whipped through all those present. It was a clear, very chilly March night and the small group of twenty bystanders, composed mainly of newspaper and radio men, as well as several UFO investigators (including rep-

Warren and Libby-Collins Frieberg try to contact via telepathy the UFO entities who were said to be landing on a regular basis in New Jersey's North Bergen Park.

presentatives of the Mutual UFO Network and Dr. Hynek's Center for UFO Studies) were huddled together for added warmth to protect themselves against the less-than pleasant elements. In the midst of the group Libby Frieberg sat on the hard, gravel-covered roof, her eyes tightly shut. She was beginning to inhale deeply and was starting to mutter in a low monotone voice. Apparently something was about to happen, for Libby's face — pleasant and normal-looking moments before — was now taking on an almost non-human appearance.

Holding tightly onto his wife's wrists, Warren instructed Libby to concentrate on "inner space, outer space, the vastness of inner and outer space." Within minutes, it was as if her vocal chords had been "taken over", by some outside entity. Gasping for air and having some difficulty speaking, a being who identified itself as *Caldon,* started to converse in a weird, metallic-sounding voice, almost as if coming from a mechanical device. The conversation lasted for approximately five minutes, during which time Warren quizzed Caldon repeatedly, extracting some startling revelations.

Q: Where are you from?

A: From here.

Q: Where is that — New Jersey? *(Warren's voice is incredulous.)*

A: From another dimension.

Q: And why have you repeatedly visited this area and collected soil samples?

A: You are misusing your environment *(the answer coming almost inaudibly).*

Q: Is that the reason you are collecting soil, as a symbolic sign?

A: Your environment is our environment . . .

Q: Okay, we understand it is the same, but Caldon, why have you come to Hudson Park?

A: To see how much time is left.

Q: To see how much time is left for people? What do you intend to do with the knowledge you're gathering?

A: We will return en masse to warn your people that if you do not stop your present way, time will be short for all of us.

Q: Caldon, what is the name of your people? What group of people do you represent?

A: We are called the Gropalins.

Q: Where are you now, physically?

A: We are here, but *not* here.

Q: You are aboard a spaceship?

A: *We are in another dimension.*

Little by little, Freiberg began to pull Libby out of her altered state explaining that "it isn't a good idea to leave any entity in charge for too long a time."

NUCLEAR PEARL

Though this episode was fairly well publicized at the time, ecological warning of one type or another are not that rare from space beings. Donn Shallcross a West Virginia construction worker says he went out one night in his darkened pasture and encountered a strange figure standing by a power pole dressed in a tight fitting uniform with a helmet covering his face, and a rod about the size of a baseball bat in his hands.

Eventually breaking their tense silence, the being who was standing near the dimly lit opening to a space craft, revealed during a rather lengthy conversation a warning that humankind was not making the best use of their natural resources and that atomic power should be used for peaceful purposes and not for war. He added that nuclear waste was very bad for our ecology and offered a harmless way of disposing of it which involved a series of pyramid-like symbols which flashed through the witnesses mind.

Back as far as the early 1950's, the UFO contactees were warning of the potential dangers of nuclear power, based upon "inner perceptions" and what they had been told by their space contacts, who they said were highly advanced, spiritual, beings. They saw greed and corruption as the root of a great deal of evil, and prophecised that the End Times were close at hand. I find it fascinating that many New Agers today are not at all familiar with the roots of their beliefs. It should be emphasized, that the messages received from the UFOnauts — or Space Brothers — frequently dealt with such esoteric subjects as earth changes, the raising of ones consciousness, healing, crystal energy, the existence of Atlantis, how the pyramids were levitated into place, and the karmic laws that govern the reincarnation of our soul.

Hundreds of books have, in the last several years, been written on these topics, and they now go to make up the popular New Age sections of book stores, where before such literary ravings were limited to a few dusty shelves marked "Occultism."

Wilbur B. Smith was, however, no "occultist" despite research which carried him into the borderland regions of phychics, philosophy and religion. He was, instead, an engineer, a scientist, a futurist, and a holder of over 40 patents, who in 1939 joined the Department of Transport of Canada and became recognized for having advanced the technical aspects of broadcasting throughout North America.

In December, 1950, Smith was authorized and received permission to make use of the Department of Transport's laboratory and field facilities in a study of UFOs and their physical flight capabilities. Not only did Smith actually track a UFO over Canadian air space, but he later became a channel for the UFO beings themselves, receiving beneficial information that he, in turn, released to a limited audience as head of the Ottawa New Sciences Club. And while he died prematurely on December 27, 1962, what Smith had to say remains important, as it deals with the intervention of space craft in our atmosphere. As we enter a new phase we will experience heavy changes in our life style, and in the things we *think* we know about the universe, and other dimensions that exist all around us.

Smith knew a great deal about the space people's plans for Earth, and in particular about their concern for our safety as far as nuclear energy is concerned. This can be attested to in the following statement made by Smith shortly before his death:

"It was explained (by the space people) that the explosion of nuclear devices (a negative force) has not only torn parts of Earth's protective atmosphere (which, if continued, may have drastic physical consequences to Man on Earth, involving violent weather patterns, floods, earthquakes and deformed biological mutations caused by increased radioactivity, etc.), but these massive explosions have, by their negative nature, also damaged the *metaphysical* protective "envelope" surrounding this planet thus allowing negative astral entities to penetrate through these ripped portions and further influence negative thinking on Earth — hence much of the trouble and strife we were experiencing in our world today. While the cosmic police force can shield us from unwarranted *outside* negative influences, they cannot protect us from the consequences of negative emanations coming directly from our own planet. This would be contrary to the universal law of karma. Only *we* can repair the damage we have created ourselves. This, say our space friends, we can do by sincere prayer for the cessation of nuclear explosions and positive thought envisualizing the closing of the gaps in our protective atmosphere and its metaphysical counterpart. Such a spiritual emanation from Earth would take the outward form of radiant light with which the space brothers claim that, with our expressed desire to do so, they could mend the torn portions of our atmosphere and thus block further entry of negative forces. They call on us urgently to play our part in an all-out effort to save ourselves and our planet from the total destruction it is otherwise headed for. Time is running short and we must act *now*."

We shall be hearing more from this great man in the pages just up ahead.

A VISITOR AT THE UN

The same basic "message" seems to be put across time after time all over the world. Usually it is received by psychic means, normally through a channel who while in an altered state of consciousness is acting as a telepathic "receiver" from some other-worldly source. Other times the message is delivered in person as was the case over a decade ago when a Mexican doctor was actualy flown to the United Nations in New York to tell his amazing story. Those present included the Ambassador of Grenada, Francis Redhead, the Assistant Secretary for Science and Technology of the UN, Joao F. Da Costa and the officer in charge of the UN's Technology Applications Section, Bertrand Chatel. Together, they entertained the M.D. from Mexico, and though the story he told might have — on the surface — seemed "far out", all indications are that the UN representatives took what the man had to say quite seriously.

During October of 1975 a gigantic "mothership" hovered over the city of Guadalajara in Central Mexico. Cars were stalled, and it is reported that hundreds of people watched the huge, sleek craft as it glided over a nearby mountain range. There were additional sightings at the time, and it was said that Mexico was experiencing "UFO fever."

During the peak of the UFO activity, an established doctor in Guadalajara found himself confronted by a most unusual patient, who had come to the doctor's office and asked to see him at once, being "seriously ill."

Ushered into the doctor's private quarters, the man complained of feeling fatigued, and asked that he be given a complete physical examination.

The doctor told the stranger to strip to the waist and he would check him over to see what was causing his condition.

As the patient unbuttoned his shirt, the doctor noticed that the color of the man's skin was unusually pink, almost like that of a child's. He also noted that there was not a single hair on the upper portion of his body (face, underarms, chest included) save for that on his head. Taking his stethoscope, he listened to the heartbeat of his patient, but could find no irregularity.

At this point the doctor requested that the man strip totally. When he was completely naked, the doctor again noticed the fact that his patient was entirely hairless — the area around his genitals looked as if they have been shaven clean. In actuality there were not even *hair follicles* on any part of his body, something that is completely unknown to biology on this planet.

With this, the man apologized for his action, saying, "I wanted to show you that I am not one of your kind." Then he started talking about the vastness of the universe, life on other planets, and the reality of UFOs. He said that alien beings from other planets had been coming to our world on a regular basis, and that the UFOnauts were worried about earth people being "so slow in your development."

They conversed for a brief period, during which time the doctor was told things of a technical nature that apparently he had no way of knowing on his own. After their talk and the examination, the doctor was utterly convinced that the man in his office was actually an alien, so much so that he felt it his duty to report the incident to "someone in authority." Ambassador Redhead of Grenada was called in to investigate the matter, and so convinced was he of the doctor's claim, that the doctor was invited to UN headquarters to tell his story.

A STRANGER'S WARNING

Anyone at all familiar with UFO and metaphysical lore will recognize right away that warnings of impending danger have often been delivered by perfect strangers. Even the Bible freely gives us several accounts of "angels" arriving to tell deserving individuals to "leave town" before disaster strikes.

Sam Alfieri, of Bishop, Calif., still recalls the visitor who called on him one day back in 1965. And while the story is over two decades old it has great relevance even more so today.

"At about 9:30 A.M. one morning, there was a knock on my door, and there stood a stranger whom I'd never seen before. He introduced himself as "Lloyd Brown." He told me he had just come from Hope Troxell's apartment in Independence, Calif., which is 42 miles south of Bishop. Hope Troxell was a channel for the space people for 26 years before her death in 1978. I said to him something like, "A friend of Hope Troxell's is a friend of mine. Come on in." He seemed to have a peaceful and friendly countenance, so I wasn't afraid to let him into my home.

"He sat in a chair and began talking to me about general things and how bad the world situation was getting to be. He seemed to be in a hurry, so he only stayed for about an hour. But before he left, he told me to get my Bible out. He referred me to the book of Jeremiah and told me to look up a certain scripture. After reading it I had a better understanding of it. He left shortly thereafter. I noticed he was driving what appeared to be a 1957 model car. After he left, I felt within myself that I was in the presence of a superior being. I've had some earlier contacts with space people while living in Southern California, but I couldn't ever be sure until now.

"The following month on May 17th, he put in another appearance. This time he stayed for three hours. He came at 4 P.M. and left at 7.

During the course of our conversation, HE SEEMED TO KNOW MORE ABOUT ME, THAN I KNEW ABOUT MYSELF! I began to wonder about this stranger. I felt for certain at this point that I was in the presence of one of the "Brothers" from space. At one point, he ordered me to get on my knees and praise the Lord. I got on my knees with my elbows on the sofa, and began praising the Lord. I must have repeated these praises about 500 times when he said to me, "That's enough, you may be seated."

"Before he left, he gave me a rather personal message. He said in part that my children and I would be taken up soon. He also indicated that some disaster would occur where people would be "living in tents and under trees. Great multitudes. It is advisable to go at least 100 miles as quickly as possible to the North and through tactful efforts in all media, to CIRCULATE THE TRUTH OF PERILOUS CONDITIONS that are rapidly forthcoming upon the planet earth." He told me that as much food as can be purchased, should be stored to feed the multitudes of truth seekers, guided to this perfection center. "It will be impossible to store more food than will be needed," he said.

"My eight year old daughter and my six year old son were present during this second visit as they both were home from school. The following year, a friend of mine came to visit. I recounted to him the story about the stranger who called himself, Lloyd Brown. My friend gave a chuckle and said, "Oh, I've heard of him, he's also been giving messages to other people." This remark was further proof to me, that I was indeed visited by a space friend who gave assurance to people that they would be removed from the Earth in time of great trouble and stress. For this we should be thankful."

As we shall see, this talk of being "removed" from our world — or lifted into a higher vibration — has become quite popular. Is it just an updated version of "Resurrection Day" or should it be taken very literally?

VISIONS OF THE "SPACE BROTHERS"
When UFOs were first seen canvassing the heavens back in the late 1940's, many people thought our planet was being invaded by

aliens from outer space. Our concept of other-worldly visitors as flesh eating, slave masters, was fostered by low budget science fiction thrillers which always portrayed the occupants of flying saucers in very negative ways. Many remembered the "War of the Worlds" radio broadcast which had our depression era planet being taken over by Martians with devastating weapons.

With all these very scary impressions floating around in our mind, it's no wonder that the mere thought of ET's landing in our back yard was enough to send us running to the nearest fallout shelter.

Yet, in actuality, based upon an evaluation of all the evidence; it would seem that the majority of UFOnauts mean us no harm. If anything, in a good percentage of cases they appear genuinely interested in our well-being, even going so far as to heal some of those they have communicated with — including poor eye sight and paralysis. There is even one case I know of from South America where an elderly UFO witness grew in a third set of teeth following a close encounter. There are even a hundred or more cases in which actual communications have been established and the aliens warn that we should mend our ways, and give up our war-like behavior before we blow ourselves into ashes. Far from monsters, these beings are usually described as humanoid in appearance, with a super intelligence and a spirituality that far overshadows our puny acceptance of God's laws. Apparently, these beings have followed our Earthly religions since its inception and accept the concept of a universal creator and acknowledge Christ as our savior and protector. Yet despite the overwhelming evidence that many of these accounts are legitimate, there is an apparently organized attempt to keep the true nature of the UFO phenomena from the public. Those in authority and power refuse to acknowledge the existence of UFOs or the "Space Brothers" as these benevolent ET's have come to be identified.

In the months just past, several out-spoken ministers have pronounced their belief in UFOs and things non-worldly. Famed evangelist Rev. Billy Graham, can be counted among those coming forth. In his book "Angels: God's Secret Agents" he makes the statement that UFOs "bear striking resemblance to angelic aircraft described thousands of years ago in the Old Testament." Graham further contends that the reason UFOs are able to defy the laws of aerodynamics, is because the beings who operate these "celestial wonders" are non flesh-and-blood mortals, but instead are of a "higher order." He added that the UFO pilots — or angels — are "so glorious and impressively beautiful as to stun and amaze men who witness their presence."

Dr. Joseph Jeffers, D.D., of St. James, Missouri, doesn't try to keep it a secret that he has seen UFOs several times, both in the waking state as well as part of a vision. "In my latest vision of UFOs, I described the object as looking like a gyroscope with windows that appeared as eyes. The windows were telescopic to give the viewers (inside) a better look. In the book of the Bible, Ezekial 1:18 it says, 'The four wheels had rims and they had spokes; and their rims were full of eyes round about.' Verse 19 goes even further: 'And when the living creatures went, the wheels went with them; and when the living creatures rose from the earth, the wheels rose.' This is taken from the Revised Standard version of the Bible. In the first and second chapters of Ezekiel, in my opinion, the great prophet was referring to a UFO and its occupants."

Dr. Frank E. Stranges, president of a New Age Christian group, the International Evangelism Crusades (Van Nuys, Calif.) goes a giant step further in that he professes to have actually met and conversed with a space being inside the Pentagon in Washington while he was speaking in that city several years ago. Rev. Stranges noticed one peculiar thing about the extraterrestrial (who looked just as human as any one of us) HE HAD NO FINGERPRINTS. Asked why, the spaceman replied: "Fingerprints are a sign of fallen man. Fingerprints mark a man all through his life. On the planet where I come from there is no crime and so there is no need for such identification." The alien, who wore a business suit when Frank met with him, added his own belief in God: "A long time ago, God looked over onto this earth and saw that the wickedness of men was very great. God, being a God of love as well as a God of justice, took upon Himself the form of a man and was born of the virgin, Mary. He succeeded in bringing man a plan of redemption through His precious blood. Everywhere Jesus went, He was doing good. In the midst of all His goodness, kindness and love, He was falsely accused, mercilessly condemned, and nailed to a cross. Even though He healed the sick, cleansed the leper, and even raised the dead, none of this was taken into consideration. They crucified He that came into this world to save sinners. And you ask me what do I think of Jesus? I know that Jesus is the alpha and omega of yours and everyone's faith. He today has assumed His rightful position as the ruler of the universe and is preparing a place and a time for all who are called by His name to ascend far above the clouds to where His power and authority shall never again be disputed. I believe that Jesus is the wonder of wonders and changes not. No, not forever and forever." Clearly words of a divine prophet as spoken by a man from another planet.

Recently, we have begun to see a marked increase in the number of letters from those who have had dreams or visions regarding the times we live in. There is a "gut feeling" among many that we are already in the "Last Days" spoken of in the Bible. Many of these seemingly inspired revelations deal with UFOs and their part in the events of the immediate future. The feeling is that UFOs somehow tie in with the "Second Coming" and the rapture in which deserving souls will be taken off this planet.

Some of the accounts we have heard are admittedly "utterly startling" in their implications, and all we can say is that such experiences seem to be increasing in frequency to the point where it would be hard to deny their validity.

Take for example, the story told to me by a young man who had just arrived in New York from Africa. Just by accident I struck up a conversation with him at a party. I was interested in knowing just how popular UFOs might be where he came from. "There's very little about them printed in the papers," he acknowledged, "but people do talk about them in private, but only with those who share their sense of knowledge."

Since coming to the United States, the young man began to have a series of odd dreams which he only told me about because of the nature of our conversation. "Funny you should mention about

UFOs," he smiled. "About two months ago I woke up in a cold sweat. In my dream, I had heard all this noise down on the street and from my loft window I could see cars jamming the intersection as far as the eye could see. I took the elevator downstairs to see what was going on. The sidewalks were packed with people pushing each other as if in a mad scramble to find out what was happening, but I also got shoved aside." The man said he got the distinct impression that the dream had something to do with Russia or China and a war. "Suddenly, the sky got brighter and looking up I saw this diamond-shaped object approaching over the tall buildings until it got closer and closer, eventually hovering overhead."

At this point, the dream always ends, but the dreamer feels that the UFO has arrived just in the nick of time as a friend and not a foe. "Why am I having this nightmare?", he wants to know. If it weren't important it would not repeat itself so often.

Two different Canadians have recently written in with frightening nightmares they have repeatedly had. One of the readers (letter on file for verification) says that he was on the street in his dream when these missiles shot overhead directed at twenty "target cities." He also observed a fleet of thirty cigar-shaped space ships filling the sky. "I sensed that a high intelligence was in command and that they were sent by God." There was another episode in which "a large, heavy, dark cloud charged with bright round nuclear fireballs contaminates everything to ground level."

Mr. Lorne Johnson of Subury, Ontario says that he had a vision a long time ago that has stuck in his mind. "In vision I saw these ships — UFOs — in the air and the world was at war. When these objects came down a 'fear' came into all the soldiers and they stopped their killing. They saw that the weapons they were fighting with were small to what 'they' had, and it made them think they would all die if they did not stop the battle. In short, man knew he was doing wrong and he feared for his inner soul."

One of the most sensational letters of this nature I've received came after an ad appeared in the National Enquirer. "Is there some way I can contact the author of *Psychic & UFO Revelations in the Last Days*," Donna S. of Sparks, Nevada wanted to know, "because some of the statements in the ad for this book closely parallel a segment of dreams that came to me late in 1971."

Donna gives this fascinating narration which covers a period of nine years: "In the fall, near sundown I left my sister's house which sat only 300 yards or so from my own. I have no memory from that point on until I awoke in my own bed near daylight, terribly ill and with the strange sensation that I'd been spinning through cold air, hanging onto some sort of metal brace and feeling very scared.

"I kept a detailed diary of the dreams that were to follow, there were lists of things to do, a specific geographic diagram of a place I was to find and a special garden that I was to plant, harvest and preserve.

"It wasn't until seven years later that something else happened. This time it included my ten year old daughter who'd gone into town with me around ten in the morning. Neither of us remember anything from the time I drove out of the driveway until nearly sundown that same night. We ended up in a town we'd never been to before, nearly 130 miles away.

"My husband thought I was going nuts not remembering what I'd done or where I'd gone, and that our daughter was helping to cover up something.

"As with the first experience, I became ill again and so did my daughter. She developed a rash on her hair line that slowly spread over her scalp and neck. I developed severe swelling in my right arm which had to be operated on in November, 1979, and she had to be operated on for several lumps that wouldn't go away in her throat that December.

"Several months after that we moved to another state where we came across an offer to buy ten acres of land. The moment I saw it I knew it was the place in my dreams, the latitude, altitude, direction from the nearest town — it all matched.

"Later, I took out some drawings I'd made. It was as though I'd stood on that very spot to draw them. It was then that I put my diary into manuscript form. Writing down every event as it had appeared to me and vividly described the very last week up to the very moment that the long silver ships with the thin red line on their sides, come down to collect the chosen.

"It was during the last week that the earth's crust began to crumble into itself and the air was thick with sulphur that rushed out of the ground, forming masses of greenish, yellowish clouds, that the sun wouldn't penetrate for hours at a time.

"As the oceans seeped over the land, hundreds of thousands were dying everywhere. They played the last rites over and over again all over the world on every radio and TV station. I lived these things as if it had already happened."

So ends Donna's vision of peril in which a certain number of people will be taken away by UFOs at the "last moment" just before the world destroys itself.

Far from being "evil sorcerers," some have made the occupants of UFOs out to be, they could be truly "messengers of light,' as the above stories clearly illustrate. Instead of being fearful of them perhaps we should seek their help and advice.

Back as far as the early 1950's, many of the UFO contactees were warning of the potential dangers of nuclear power, corrupted by greed and out of control. And while many New Agers today may not be overly familiar with the roots of their beliefs, it should be pointed out that the Space Brothers through the many UFO witnesses who they supposedly met and conversed with (often while going for a ride inside these outer space craft) frequently spoke of such esoteric matters as coming earth changes, the raising of vibrations, healing powers, the importance of crystals in our life, the existence of Atlantis, how the pyramids came to be built, and the importance of dreams in relationship to these subjects.

CHAPTER THREE

Psychic & UFO Revelations

I t is not our purpose to validate psychic phenomena or even such simple matters as the reality of extrasensory perception. Most of those "open minded" enough to purchase such a book as this, must already be familiar with the valuable research done by investigators such as the late Prof. J.B. Rhine of Duke University.

Taking into consideration the fact that UFO pilots and crew members must be "light years" beyond where we stand on the evolutionary scale, it stands to reason that their psychic abilities would have progressed to the point where they are able to accomplish almost any feat. Situated in various countries around the world are highly sensitive earthlings who are able to "tune in" to the wave lengths of these alien beings and actually act as sort of a "radio receiver" in picking up messages that are being "beamed" from beyond our atmosphere. Some of this information is taken down in the form of automatic writing, but usually the man or woman actually allows his vocal cords to be taken over so that there is no chance for human error or misinterpretation.

The majority of "sermons" which have been delivered through these "Channels" as they are often referred to, deal with upcoming events and trends on earth, primarily geological, meteroligical and political. What makes it quite obvious that no fraud is being committed by these "Channels" is the fact that the messages are all similar even though they are "beamed" to vastly separate parts of the world. Also beyond mere coincidence is the astounding fact that the extraterrestrials who are extending their hand in friendship, almost always have the same names. Names that keep cropping up over and over again in such communications include Monka, Mohada, Deska, and most popular of all, Ashtar. It is repeatedly stated that Ashtar is in charge of thousands of space ships as well as the "Commander of ten million space men, now occupying bases established within range of your planet." Some of the beings who are making themselves heard are supposedly human just as we are — flesh and blood creatures — while others have rid themselves of their physical bodies and now exist in a sort of computerized form. These entities of vast knowledge are said to travel from solar system to solar system in huge "Mother Ships" but sometimes they actually take up residence on other planets which orbit around our sun. For according to these channels, believe it or not, there is supposedly intelligent life on Venus, Mars, Jupiter, Saturn and so forth — this, despite what astronomers and other scientists might have to say. Though some of this life may be in the solid form such as we humans, many of these beings are said to exist on higher levels of vibration and in other dimensions which are normally invisible to the human eye.

We will not try to sway your beliefs. We simply ask that you read the information that is being passed along and judge for yourself its validity. We ask nothing but your attention and a promise that you will study this material carefully for your own benefit, and not for ours.

WHY THEY COME AND WHAT IT IS THEY WANT

"They do not wish to cause us any harm. They don't care to be recognized or hassled by people, and so they frequently share helpful information through mental telepathy," acknowledges psychic Bertie Catchings of Dallas, Texas, who is highly thought of in her community, having assisted families and law officers in over 50 crime-related cases.

The psychic says that aliens are working in hospitals, as well as energy-related fields, space technology and in various jobs related to science. Their characteristics include being very efficient, above average in intelligence, easy to get along with, and they never ask questions ex-

Psychic Bertie Catchings of Dallas, Texas.

cept about their duties. They look like earth people and include the entire spectrum of race characteristics and color. They dress simply, with very little jewelry except a watch. They need little sleep, and they always seem to be in excellent health. Sometimes they have brown markings on their hands and arms that form star patterns. Their purpose is to study earth in order to gain knowledge that will be helpful to the entire universe. For instance, the people of earth have many illnesses that are caused by the pollution of air and water. Most of earth's problems are not experienced on other planets — they can prevent them from happening by studying our mistakes.

THE BATTLE FOR MAN'S MIND

Some time ago, Wilbur Smith figured out that Earth was more-or-less a "battle ground." The Canadian scientist, and Channel for information from space, saw our globe as being pulled upon in a cosmic "tug-of-war" between the forces of good and evil. He saw this conflict — taking place in this dimension as well as on other planes — coming to a final conclusion before the year 2,000 is over.

"I propose," declared Smith, "to give a warning of grave danger which we are all, consciously or unconsciously, facing in a world in which two great forces are striving to gain control of man's mind. This struggle has been going on from time immemorial, but never in the world's history has the conflict been more intense than it is in this present era of confusion and unrest. In the old days, mankind was often made to suffer physically, unspeakable things in the name of power, but today, with man's mind more developed and better educated, he is now facing the prospect of a refinement of even greater mental and spiritual cruelty — unless he is prepared to protect himself with right thinking.

The two great forces involved in trying to influence man's thinking may be described as *positive,* i.e., thoughts in harmony with the concept of a love of God and the brotherhood of man, and *negative,* those encompassing anti-Christ motives designed to gain control over man for the purpose of power. This battle for Man's mind is being waged on two fronts, the physical and the metaphysical, and the object of the fight is to bring about either the spiritual salvation or destruction of homo sapiens."

Apparently, Smith determined that UFOs were most important in Earth's overall spiritual development, especially as relates to the End Times.

"We may summarize the entire flying saucer picture as follows. We have arrived at a time in our development when we must make a final choice between right and wrong. The people from elsewhere are much concerned about the choice which we will make, partly because it will have its repercussions on them and partly because we are their blood brothers and are truly concerned with our welfare. There is a cosmic law against interfering in the affairs of others, so they are not allowed to help us directly even though they could easily do so. We must make our own choice of our own free will. Present trends indicate a series of events which may require the help of these people and they stand by ready and willing to render that help. In fact, they have already helped us a great deal, along lines which do not interfere with our freedom of choice. In time, when certain events have transpired, and we are so oriented that we can accept these people from elsewhere, they will meet us freely on the common ground of mutual understanding and trust, and we will be able to learn from them and bring about the Golden Age all men everywhere desire deep within their hearts."

A true New Age visionary, Smith fully realized that "which is hidden from view" often is as important as that which we can see with our eyes. Thus he turned his thoughts to other planes and realms in order to fully understand that which is at play in the universe as concerns our way of life in the years just ahead.

"Messages received through esoteric sources, purporting to come from Space Brothers who take an active interest in the spiritual welfare of the inhabitants of our planet, warn us that an even greater conflict is being fought on the metaphysical plane where intelligent beings of both a higher and a lower spiritual order than themselves are waging a fierce battle for Man's mind. The lower or negative forces, damned themselves by wrong thinking, are projecting strong thoughts Earthward in an attempt to bring about our spiritual downfall. On the other hand, Space Brothers and other spiritual guardians of our planet, are concentrating equally hard on sending out positive thoughts of goodwill and brotherly love. Thus we are being bombarded from the metaphysical plane by two conflicting schools of thought, and, free will being the criterion of spiritual advancement, it is left to us which we choose to accept. However, from a purely logical point of view, if we want to save ourselves a lot of sorrow both in this life and lives to come, we should arm ourselves mentally against the onslaught of negative thoughts.

"This is no time for confused or apathetic thinking — often the future breeding-ground of negative thoughts. Nor should we be just receivers and disseminators of the thoughts we pick up. Rather, we should get on the transmitting end and constantly project positive thoughts of goodwill to all. Every positive thought neutralizes a negative thought, so we shall be serving not only ourselves but all humanity.

"In the final analysis, there are two simple, clear-cut maxims to be observed for complete protection from the negative forces at work on this planet: (1) Acknowledgement and love of God as the Father of all Creation, and (2) brotherly love extended to *all* His creatures throughout the universe. Anything else which interferes with these two beliefs should be vigorously rejected. Further, if we return love for hate, hate will die of malnutrition, for it can only feed on returned hatred. Let us rather pray for spiritual enlightenment for these wretched souls who seek to harm us.

"In conclusion, if any of you have doubts about the veracity of the telepathic and inspirational messages received from Space Brothers and others interested in the welfare of our planet, just ask yourselves this one vital question — 'Are these messages good and true and for the benefit of mankind on Earth?' If, as you surely must, you come up with an answer of 'Yes,' then it is obvious that it is the hand of God at work, no matter what medium He chooses to use."

TIME FOR CHANGE

Dr. Wanda M. Lockwood of Sedalia, Colorado, a student of metaphysics who holds a doctor's degree from the Brotherhood of the White Temple says that the entire Cosmos is nearing its material end, and that all intelligences from all dimensions, interlocking spaces and planets *must* at this time establish enduring harmony with one another.

Dr. Lockwood believes that we are presently 23 years into the Age of Aquarius, and that the so-called "Aliens of Light" are working very vigorously to bring Earth in perfect rapport with the rest of the universe. Dr. Lockwood maintains that included among the goals of the UFOnauts are the following principles:

1. Join earthmen as one of them.
2. Counsel and train man in higher ways.
3. Aid the peace-makers whenever danger threatens them.
4. Help prepare earth for the great trials soon to besiege this planet.
5. Aid man in evolving peace and technology.
6. Reveal high-secret knowledge to those who qualify through virtue.
7. Act as a bridge between obsolete beliefs and superstitions, to greater and true teachings and systems.
8. Help establish Universal Brotherhood, total acceptance and understanding of all species, regardless of form or culture.
9. Aid man in re-awakening his 6th sense, the sense which acts as

his preserver of harmony and peace.

10. Teach the secrets of immortality and eternal youth.

11. Teach man how to manipulate the fixed Universe Laws.

Dr. Lockwood is convinced that the main reason we are being visited at this time, is due to the fact that the UFOnauts are "helping to prepare man for the last great catastrophe. It's very near now," she states. "Possibly, within the next 15 years, or it may even occur much sooner, before 1985. The exact time is unknown. It may involve a devastating global war or vast earthquakes, or possibly a combination of quakes triggered by mighty nuclear weapons."

TYPICAL ALIEN IMAGE

UFOnauts are able to walk the Earth undetected, supposedly because they look so human. Dr. Wanda M. Lockwood did this drawing.

Others who have studied all the available information feel pretty much the same way. For example, Laura Mundo, who runs the Flying Saucer Information Center in Inkster, Michigan believes that alien beings are trying to help us to help ourselves, "before the atmosphere becomes unbearable due to increased sunspot activity, which is creating extremes in weather, people's actions, natural catastrophes and causing confusion in general."

Like many other psychics, UFO contactees and New Age channels we have conversed with, Laura is of the opinion that the UFO-nauts are here to help us through a

Pictured in front of a bell-shaped saucer that George Adamski photographed, Laura Mundo says the same type of craft passed over her home in Sept., 1955.

period of great crisis. "Those who *qualify*," she states, "will be taken to a place of safety in the space people's insulated ships, through the unbelievable planetary turmoil, and come back after the sunspots settle down." Laura says that as far back as 1955 she received a message on her shortwave radio from a spaceman telling her that time was short for mankind. She is convinced this message is coming true today.

Almost every clairvoyant we have communicated with agrees that these changes are going to happen, though they insist there is no way of telling how extreme they will be. There are even some who insist the planet will become uninhabitable for years to come because of an axis shift which will send our planet into another orbit and change the climates on the planet.

I have more or less concluded that this information is valid and that our time is limited here on earth. What I have tried to determine through my own research efforts is who will be taken from this planet and how we should make ourselves ready. I have tried to gather as much specific information as possible and through this book I am passing this information on to you. I ask that you share it with all those who will listen.

The late archaeologist and UFOlogist Dr. George Hunt Williamson sums it up eloquently when he said:

"Many so-called prophets today are foretelling horrible destruction and doom for the people of Earth. They claim life is eternal, yet they fear the transition called 'death'. The space friends are here to help us, not to destroy us . . . and although there are going to be vast changes taking place from time to time on the physical, mental and spiritual planes, still only the good is to be inherited by man on this sorrowful planet!

Earthman has reached the stage in his evolution where he must be shown that he is not merely a lonely accident on one world only. His brothers and sisters exist on literally billions and billions of worlds in the Omniverse! As we come more and more under the beneficent rays of Aquarius, cosmic-ray bombardment will become more intensified and EVERYTHING on our planet will be changed vibrationally.

For centuries, Theology has battled Science, and vice versa. What they are arguing about is not known, for the two are really one, and will become one in the 'Golden Dawn' approaching rapidly. All former theories will be discarded . . . or at least improved upon. We will know definitely where we have been inaccurate in the past and why! Truth will not contradict Truth. Therefore our Philosophy of Life will be built on a science that recognizes a Creator of the Cosmos and a Divine Plan working everywehre!

No longer will we be required to follow certain ritualistic practices or believe certain dogma in order to get into "heaven". On the other hand, we will no longer have to swing to the other side of the road to embrace the cold, bare facts of materialistic science. In short, we are about to 'level off' or 'get in balance'.

Matters are what they are because of certain unstable or unbalanced conditions on the Earth planet. With the help of our space friends we are about to enter a 'Golden Age', but it won't happen by the time you read this article. We are even now in transition and it won't be very long before those thought to be 'psychic fanatics', will find they are no longer in the minority! Call this New Age a new dispensation, a Golden Dawn or Age, a new density or dimension or Aquarius . . . it really doesn't matter . . . the important thing is . . . IT IS HERE!''

CHAPTER FOUR

And The Earth Shall Tremble

I n 1934 the Sleeping Prophet of Virginia Beach, Edgar Cayce, uttered the following words while in a sleep-like state:

"THE EARTH WILL BE BROKEN UP IN MANY PLACES, THE EARLY PORTION WILL SEE A CHANGE IN THE PHYSICAL ASPECT OF THE WEST COAST OF AMERICA...THE EARTH WILL BE BROKEN UP IN THE WESTERN PORTION OF AMERICA...AND THESE CHANGES WILL BEGIN IN THOSE PERIODS IN FIFTY-EIGHT TO NINETY-FIVE...LOS ANGELES, SAN FRAN-CISCO, MOST ALL OF THESE WILL BE AMONG THOSE THAT WILL BE DESTROYED — BEFORE NEW YORK EVEN."

Cayce repeatedly claimed that he foresaw a complete upheaval that would change the course of the Mississippi and put both the coast of Southern California and New York City beneath water. He saw in conjunction with this wide spread disruption of land masses an increase in earthquakes, volcanic eruptions and freak weather conditions. Cayce, as well as many other seers who voiced their opinions in the years that followed, said this upheaval would start to flare

up in the latter part of the 1970's, and increase in strength throughout the decade to come.

What makes the predictions of these psychics so frightening is
the fact that the world of science has also been talking of such events
that could easily alter the geography of this planet.

SUPER STORMS PREDICTED

Recently, Howard Sargent of the Space Environment Services
Center located in Boulder, Colorado made a startling announcement.
He predicted that in the next few years our planet would probably
be struck by magnetic "super storms" that could cause unprecedented electrical blackouts. There would be extended periods
where we would be unable to receive or send radio signals, thus disrupting our communications systems on a world wide basis.

You do not have to be a genius to realize what the outcome of
such a fierce storm might be. The planet would be thrown into utter chaos, and if they wanted, this would be an opportune time for
our enemies to attack. Radar scopes would go blank. Military bases
around the world would be unable to contact each other. Emergen-
cy information could not be broadcast. We would be at the mercy
of those who are dead set against us. There is little way of telling
what the end result might be, but it probably wouldn't be good!

The Space Environment Services Center spokesman explained
that these storms would be due to increased sunspot activity and
that at this moment, the sun is giving off powerful outbursts called solar flares. Sargent says that the blackouts will happen when
magnetic disruptions (caused by these solar flares) set up currents
in power transmission lines that cause overloads and eventually cut
off power.

Other scientists who carefully chart our weather conditions maintain that there is likely to be extensive change in our climate partly due to the changing jet stream as well as the eruption of Mount
St. Helens, which spewed volcanic ash high into the atmosphere
blocking out heat giving rays from the sun.

If you think that storms result in a few uprooted trees, some
smashed windows and downed power lines, you've obviously not

familiar with the fury a bad storm can bring with it. In recent years there have been more hurricanes and freak rain storms than ever before. The house pictured in the above photo was actually turned on its side after a disastrous flood hit the Wilkes-Barre, Pennsylvania area following the arrival of Hurricane Agnes. The total damage from this storm was over $23 million, and extended over an area of 12 states.

So again we're jolted into seeing that what psychics and UFO channels have been predicting is now taking place and has been confirmed by our scientific community. These things are no longer to be joked at, but should constitute serious business for those of us who need to know when we are to "pull up stakes" and head to more secure regions which the space beings say will be "safe," at least for a short period of time.

Scientists say that we will see extremes of both hot and cold. Although this condition is going to get even worse, already we have seen dozens of elderly people dying from temperatures of 100 degrees which struck several states for weeks and months upon end with no let up in sight.

Dr. Reid A. Bryson, Professor of Meteorology and director of the Institute of Environmental Studies at the University of Wisconsin, has gone on record as saying that within the next few years there may be glacial conditions in America. "Winters in the South will continue to get colder. Heavy snow will be common in the once-sunny South. Northern Florida might even be snowbound." He continues by noting that the main feature of our weather will be the way it will jump around like crazy. "New Orleans for example, might be bitterly cold one year and mild the next."

Another expert, Dr. Murray Mitchell Jr., project scientist at the National Oceanic and Atmospheric Administsration, has said: "It is quite possible that we are headed for a more severe climate than any in recent history."

We emphasize such conditions because for many years, psychics have been predicting that strange weather patterns would be the order of the day as we approach the End Times. UFO channels have been coming up with similar information dating back to the early 1950's when so-called "Super Storms" were never even dreamed of, much less a reality.

MORE U.S. VOLCANOES COULD BLOW THEIR STACK

Nobody could have been more shocked and surprised than the residents of the state of Washington when Mount St. Helens blew her stack spewing potent and lethal volcanic ash high above the earth. There hadn't been a volcanic eruption in the continental United States since May 30, 1914, when Lassen Peak (Calif.) went off.

Recently, scientists have begun to warn that our luck may be running out. The photo on the following page, taken in Iceland after a volcanic eruption paints a rather sobering picture of how molten lava can flow from an active volcano and cover an entire town up to the tops of homes in a matter of no time at all. Human life has been known to have been exterminated for miles around following such an eruption, as was the case when Mount St. Helens exploded. As an example of this wide spread devastation, in 1902 a volcano erupted on the island of Martinique, sending deadly "fireballs" into the air. More than 35,000 individuals were killed in the Mount Pelee eruption, most of them in the span of less than a minute.

In addition to Mount St. Helens which has gone off several times already and is still potentially dangerous, the Division of Volcanology at the Smithsonian Institution in Washington, D.C. list the following seven volcanoes as still being active, though they are dormant at this particular moment.

* MT. HOOD, OREGON
* MT. RAINIER, WASHINGTON
* MT. BAKER, CALIFORNIA
* LASSEN PEAK, CALIFORNIA
* MOUNT SHASTA, CALIFORNIA
* MAUNA LOA, HAWAII
* KILAUEA, HAWAII

Taking the predictions of the psychics we have talked with about the End Times seriously, as well as what the Space Brothers have to say, you can almost bet that several of the above listed volcanoes will shoot their top off in the not too distant future. Such eruptions on the "Cosmic Clock" are slated to begin happening right now, as such eruptions are said to be one of the signs that the worst is still to come.

STRANGE EARTHQUAKES IN OUT OF THE WAY PLACES

As man continues to do his best to rape the planet and take advantage of Mother Nature's delicate balance, there is every indication that our heavenly body is reacting in a very negative way, threatening to get rid of every last person who would poison it. In an article published in the first issue of a very stimulating magazine entitled "Future Times & Predictions" the author of a feature story called "Shakedown," makes the observation that: "Man has been blamed as the cause of earthquakes, for when he builds dams, drills for oil or pumps waters underground, he exerts much the same sort of pressure as molten rock does on the earth's crust. If you find this hard to believe, consider the recent study that showed that more earthquakes occur near large dams than in any other areas of the world. Or consider the fact that, in the 1960s, the first earthquakes in history were recorded in Denver, after the U.S. Army began dumping lethal wastes nearby. When residents starting filing lawsuits against the army for the damage done by the numerous quakes, the army discontinued dumping, and the quakes came to a halt as suddenly and mysteriously as they began. Want more? In 1978, after the Soviet Union ran several underground nuclear tests, an earthquake shook Iran that killed 25,000 people. Several European seismologists remain convinced that it was those underground explosions that precipitated the earthquakes."

One observer of End Times phenomenon, Jon Douglas Singer, M.A. who lives in New Haven, Conn., has been keeping careful track of recent tremors, and is convinced earthquakes are on the increase not only just in the places where they usually occur but in places where they seldom cause damage.

The following is an exclusive report on his findings.

Certain areas of the country are more prone to quakes than others (above).

Giant quakes have hit Calif. before. During the early part of this century tremors shook San Francisco. Buildings fell to the ground and fires started.

Most people usually think that earthquakes occur mainly in four areas: California and nearby regions in the Southwest along the San Andreas Fault; Latin America; the Mediterranean region, and Asia (especially in the Middle East and in Central Asia). However, earthquakes also occur in countries that don't usually experience such frightening events. When earthquakes such as these happen, people wonder why, and scientists are puzzled by these long dormant faults.

Many regions of the Northeastern coast of the United States, especially New England, *have* had tremors before, but not since the 1700s. From data I have recently sifted through it has become apparent that a new series of quakes has struck and threatens to happen again.

The first of the mysterious out-of-place earthquakes struck central and northern New Jersey, as well as portions of Southern New

York State (including parts of New York City), on Tuesday, March 30, 1979, as people were preparing for their noon lunch breaks or going about their regular daily routine.

Articles published in New York newspapers during that week, gave the quake the name the Cheesquake Earthquake because, oddly enough, the point at which it was strongest, was Cheesquake, New Jersey. Windows shook along a line extending from Perth Amboy in southern New Jersey to Long Island, and people reported feeling great shocks.

On May 20, 1980, Walter Sullivan of the New York Times wrote about recent research on the cause of earthquakes in the Mississippi Valley region near Missouri, western Kentucky, and Tennessee. He revealed the findings by geologist Dr. Mark Zoback of the U.S. Geological Survey and others, who have found remnants of the deeply buried "rift valley" covered by two miles of earth and rock deposited about a hundred million years ago.

The rift causes a zone of weakness which occasionally spawns earthquakes as the continental masses over it drift apart, ever so gradually, in an east-west direction. This may be the cause of the great New Madrid, Missouri, earthquake of 1811-12, which altered the course of the Mississippi slightly and formed new lakes. Other earthquakes such as the Charleston, South Carolina in 1886, were probably caused by it. This rift may have caused a subterranean chain-reaction that ultimately set off the Ramapo Fault earthquakes in New York State and southern Ontario in Canada. This happened on January 17, 1980.

Oddly enough, shortly after Sullivan's article in the New York Times, an earthquake actually did rock 11-14 Midwestern and Appalachian states which included, Kentucky, Michigan, South Carolina, Indiana, Ohio, Pennsylvania, West Virginia, Tennessee, Illinois, North Carolina, and even parts of New York state and southern Ontario.

The earthquake hit at 2:52 P.M., New York time, according to United States Geological Survey official Don Finley. He reported that the earthquake was as high as 5.1 on the Richter Scale. This is rare for the East, which very seldom has more than 4.0 level shocks. The epicenter or most powerful site of the quake was at a spot 45 miles southeast of Cincinnati. People felt their houses and radiators shaking. In fact, the quake was so strong that a Detroit Tin Tigers' baseball game was interrupted for a few minutes as fans actually noticed that the stadium swayed. Luckily nobody panicked, despite the fact that the ball park was packed with a crowd of 40,000. The announcer actually stopped the game to broadcast news of the earthquake over the P.A. system and shortly thereafter the game resumed when normality had returned. Everybody just sort of looked at each other, but showed no obvious signs of terror. Due to the level of self-control on the part of the fans, a disaster scenario was averted, considering that a stampede might have occurred in their haste to leave the stadium.

The next month, on August 20, 1980, the same area was again jarred by a quake. This one, to be sure, was less powerful but still big enough to make headlines. It measured 3.0 on the Richter Scale and took place in the wee hours of the morning at 5:35 A.M. The tremor was felt from Lake Erie to Detroit.

The next event has an aura of eeriness about it, at least for me. I was talking with a friend over the phone and we were discussing the recent earthquakes in Algeria and Mexico. I told him I thought the earth was cracking up. At that very moment, an earthquake was rumbling through my hometown of New Haven. The shock measured 3.0 and was felt in such other nearby communities as Derby, East Haven, Ellsworth, Haddam, Moodus, North Stonington, and in the city of Meriden. This was October 24, 1980, and on that same day, at 8:41 P.M. there was an additional disturbance known as an "aftershock." The dark night was shaken by a weird rumbling sound. This quake reached 2.9 on the Richter Scale. My parents, Prof. Jerome L. Singer of Yale University, and Prof. Dorothy G. Singer of the University of Bridgeport, felt a tremor rumble through their house in Woodbridge, Conn. To them it sounded "as if a boiler had been turned on." A resident of Hamden, Richard Ziemba, even saw his appliances move around slightly. Ansonia police reported that their switchboard was flooded with calls and in that town residents reportedly heard loud noises while they felt their houses shake.

Our local ABC-TV affiliate, Channel 8 Action News, reported that only minor damage occurred, when apparently several witnesses reported that their teacups and chinaware broke. They also said that residents along Quinnipiac Avenue in New Haven felt tremors. The shocks were supposedly felt even in the state capital of Hartford.

James McCaffrey of the Western Observatory, which has been studying east coast earthquakes for five years, said that this quake's strength was unusual because most of the tremors in this region are so slight that normally they are only recorded on seismographs, but aren't felt by people.

Another quake had occurred in Maine on September 8, and I even spoke with a newsstand cashier who said he felt the ground shake during an earlier episode. Scientist Vladimir Vudler has noted that earthquakes are rare in New England, and that the last ones which measured 5.0 or more all took place over 200 years ago.

The big question is why now, why today in our life time? Even scientists can't explain this mystery. One can only wonder as to the reason they occurred rather frequently in the early centuries of our nation and then resumed rather abruptly today after a long hiatus of relative quiet. It seems that even the peaceful countryside of New England hides its share of enigmas.

A POTENTIAL DANGER

While Jon Singer points out that none of these recent quakes on the east coast caused any great damage, there is a potential danger that is very real which many scientists refuse to acknowledge.

In 1976 an earthquake ran through the area near Indian Point, New York where a nuclear power plant is located. Residents who have their homes nearby were realistically concerned that the power plant might possibly develop leaks due to the tremors, and might as a result send nuclear waste — highly radioactive waste — billowing into the air. Nothing of the sort happened this time, but there's no telling when an accident such as this might happen. In particular, many residents of California are shaking in their boots day and night because reactors in their state have been constructed along the famed fault lines there, the worst in this country anywhere.

If several massive quakes were to happen on the same day in different parts of the world society would be at its wits end. Communications would be cut off to a large extent. Transportation would come to a standstill as it would be unsafe to travel. Bridges might collapse. Major highways could buckle. Train tracks may end up twisted into distorted shapes, and large crevices could make landing at airports highly dangerous. Without high speed transportation medical supplies could not reach their destinations, and food supplies would quickly be used up as meat, vegetables and fruits would never make it from the farm into our cities.

As you can see, earthquakes are no laughing matter. Millions of people have been killed in various parts of the world because they were not prepared and didn't know what course of action to take when the ground began to give out from under their feet. Much publicity has been given to the fact that California may eventually fall into the sea. Even skeptical scientists who refuse to speak of a possible doomsday, admit that the West Coast is due for a big shake. They say that this "Monster Quake" could happen at any time. Many residents of California actually have earthquake insurance and a number of people have already collected on their policies. New buildings are supposedly earthquake proof, but a big enough tremble will cause just about any structure, no matter how stable, to "give way."

THE SIDE EFFECTS SPELL DISASTER

If all the above comes to pass, people will be without homes and without food. Our drinking water will become contaminated and in all likelihood — without the availability of medicine — great plagues could sweep over our cities. In poorer countries it will be just about impossible for food supplies to reach out-of-the-way villages and cannibalism — flesh eating! — may become quite common as rice and other food staples become non-existent. Hundreds of thousands from all races and religions could perish in a matter of 48 hours and we will remain powerless to do anything to counter balance this situation as each one of us will have to fight for survival.

It becomes apparent that if the psychics, religious leaders and scientists are all correct, we will have to look elsewhere for help. No earthly power can come to our aid, but many agree assistance could be forthcoming from a "higher" source.

CHAPTER FIVE

The Evacuation

I f we should find ourselves caught up in a state of utter chaos, and there is apparently no means of escaping the disastrous situation the planet as a whole is gripped by, should we give up total hope of salvation?

The answer to this question is a definite "No!"

Those students of the Bible who take this great book literally, all know that in the Last Days, Jesus Christ will descend from Heaven, extend His hands and those who have been righteous all their lives will be saved as the world is about to go to pieces. Just about every religious sect seems to feel that they are the "chosen ones," and that when the day of atonement arrives they will be ushered up into a cloud and spirited away to a safe home far away from our trouble plagued Earth. Every group thinks they are "special" and that their adherents have been hand picked by the Lord for some special mission that will get them an honored seat in Heaven. This belief is as old as religion itself and survives today in most Christian doctrines. Evangelists the world over pound the pulpit with sermons of fire and brimstone warning that the wicked are doomed. They all seem to believe that we are living in the End Times, or a period of Great Tribulation. And, indeed, a reading of the

Book of Revelations does give indication that "troubled waters" will soon surround us on all sides. Revelations speaks openly of a world caught on fire (nuclear war?) and terrible battles which will involve millions of soldiers. Supposedly the battle of Armageddon will result in the demise of one fourth of the world's population.

Yet, despite references to "rivers of blood" and great tribulations to come, throughout the Bible we are informed that "the elect," "the chosen," — the "righteous" — will be removed in the last few minutes before life as we have come to recognize it, vanishes from the face of the earth. Interestingly enough this same belief exists in other religions besides Christianity. The North American Indian tribe, the Hopis, have long believed in a similar disaster of a magnitude that hasn't shook our planet in thousands of years. Say the Hopi prophecies:

Listen, listen, White Man, Brother,
  For the Day is close upon us.
Will the Great Massau'u return,
  Or will there come the Terrible One?

But if the Sacred Land is taken,
  Then comes the changing of the Seasons,
Earth will quake, and from the West Wind,
  There will come the Terrible One.

They shall make a little ball that will
fall to the earth, and the earth will be
devastated . . . a gourd of molten ashes
falls from out of heaven.

So this day is close upon us,
  When our Earth will shake and tremble
And the Old World, soon forgotten,
  So our land will be no more.

According to these same Hopi prophecies those "whose hearts are at peace" will be lead to safety and find refuge in a land they call Oraibi which some believe to be inside the earth.

Occult traditon holds to pretty much the same belief pattern. Over eighty years ago a massive book was transcribed by a young Californian. "A Dweller on Two Planets" was given through automatic writing from an entity known as Phylos who supposedly once existed on this planet in the days of Atlantis in an earlier incarnation and is now in the spirit world. Phylos' dire message is quite hair raising to say the least, and tells of a scorching of the earth:

> "Unto the end of full obedience and the coming into harmony with Divine Law shall the lash be applied; words may not portray the scenes (of the great holocaust). This is the message of the End of the Age. The day of vengeance is in mine heart, and the year of my redeemed is come high. Behold the day...that burneth as an oven."

Phylos reminds us that we have wandered from the Way, "cast out love and placed violence, lust and greed and all the riotous animalism in us in command of our lives." It would seem that this entity is in command of a considerable amount of knowledge regarding the End Times. He has accurately predicted what the Last Days will be like and has indicated that a nuclear explosion may do us in. His reference to "the day that burneth as an oven" is absolutely uncanny when you consider that these words were written down almost a century ago, long before any A bomb had been exploded.

What makes the remarks of Phylos even more uncanny is the fact that this material was written down in the state of California, and it is here that many psychics and scientists believe these global changes will first begin. Even more bizarre are the references made to the earth-burning, as it is also in California where forest fires have raged out of control for weeks on end. Millions of dollars in property damage have been recorded, some of the homes belonging to famous show business personalities, who find themselves just as vulnerable to Mother Nature's whims as anyone else of a lesser stature would be. Because of changes in the climate it is possible that wooded areas would remain so dry that almost anything could set this tinder box off like it were a match stick. Earthquakes could trigger off the explosion of gas mains and city after city could go up in smoke in a matter of no time. Look for such massive blazes in the Last Days. Its been predicted in the Bible as well as by psychics and the UFO channels we will be quoting throughout the remainder of this book.

MASSIVE UFO LANDINGS PREDICTED

It has been my chosen task to get to the bottom of the End Times mystery, and actually try and find out how the Last Days will arrive, and who — if, indeed, anyone — will be saved. The Bible talks of "signs and wonders" in the heavens, and I've little doubt but that the appearance of UFOs in our skies has something to do with what is referred to often in the New Testament. But what of the other "road signs" that supposedly will be offered as clues that not very much time is left for us to get our affairs in order? Just what type of

Timothy Green Beckley and channel Bob Short in front of the Solar Space Foundation's headquarters.

advance warning will be given, and most important of all, who among us now living on this planet, will be saved from certain death when the natural and man-made terrors start to take place on a regular basis?

— 58 —

The questions are many, and in order to get some answers I have traveled the highways and back roads of America speaking with those individuals who seem highly attuned to these changing times in which we now find ourselves. It became quite clear that there is an understanding among many mystics and sensitives that massive UFO landings will take place and will take up a select few just in the nick of time. This same belief is world wide and comes from many groups and individuals who claim they are receiving regular messages from highly evolved beings who reside elsewhere than our planet.

Robert Short is the curly-haired leader of an organization known as the Solar Space Foundation, located in Joshua Tree, California. Since the early 1950's, Short has been conditioned to receive information while in an altered state of consciousness. During the period when he is in a trance-like state, Short is able to act as a Channel for extraterrestrials who give hope and encouragement despite our troubled state of affairs on Earth.

According to Short, his channeling endeavors started in the early 1950's and took the form of automatic writing, but shortly thereafter the alien intelligences began to communicate with him in a much more direct way — through his voice box. "One of the things I have been told," insists Short, "is that we will some day see a mass UFO landing take place.

"As far as I can tell, there is going to be one major landing, followed by more landings, and not just our government will know about this. Many earth people of all occupations will be involved. The landing will take place in the Southwest — New Mexico, Texas or Arizona. The ship will come down in a large flat area and the craft will be anywhere from 70 to 100 feet in diameter. It will hold a mixed crew of men and women, representatives of their civilizations in space.

"The landing," Short continues, "will take place in such a fashion that they will for the first time tell the exact reasons behind their coming to our world at this time. They are coming due to extreme shifts which will start to take place in the earth's crust, causing devastating earthquakes and total disaster worldwide. In order to inform everyone of these changes they may use radio, telephones and TV to broadcast an important message over the airwaves."

It is interesting to note at this point that almost all the UFO contactees and Channels I have talked with maintain that the aliens will eventually broadcast over our airwaves in order to tell the world what is about to transpire all over the earth, and that their visits are peaceful and only meant to help us through this difficult period of time.

During the course of our conversation, Robert Short revealed that the aliens will definitely take people on board with one qualification — "They will ask that those selected avail themselves of a physical examination. A select number will be evacuated and will not be seen until after the catastrophes are over. In addition to the landing in the Southwest, other landing sites will be chosen away from the troubled fault lines. The American Indians and other knowledgeable individuals will assist in the evacuation.

"There will be a certain amount of panic," Short admits, "but because of the situation developing on earth, people will be looking for any influence that can aid them in the hours of strife ahead.

TAKEN TO A SAFE PLACE

Until they recently met, Jane Allyson did not know of Robert Short nor of his predictions concerning a mass evacuation.

Jane Allyson says there will be a mass evacuation of the planet just before great disasters plague us.

— 60 —

Neither was she aware of his vision of worldwide disaster. Yet their findings are, in many ways, similar.

"I have been a practicing psychic for several years, but have only recently gotten into space channeling," she explains. Jane had a very moving UFO experience in lower Manhattan and shortly thereafter she started to receive some rather remarkable communications which include End Time prophecies. "I've been told that there will be a landing in a large flat area of either Arizona or New Mexico," Jane says. "I have no idea of the actual number of craft that will land, but those that do touch down will be used to evacuate people into space when the earthquakes and other natural disturbances become too much to handle." In October, 1978 Jane received through automatic writing that a communications network is now being set up to assist in an evacuation. "I've also experienced a series of dreams in which I was told that at one point our sky is going to be filled up with spaceships. I was further shown that there will be much turmoil and confusion and there will be buildings collapsing. A psychic saw me climbing into a spaceship that will hold up to 300 people, and I have felt that when there is an evacuation, I will be among those to be taken off this planet."

WHAT DO UFOS HAVE PLANNED FOR HUMANITY?

When it comes to UFOs there seem to be a million unanswered questions that have to be dealt with. But taken into consideration the many varified sightings, landings, contacts and abductions it is most likely that the occupants of these craft have an overall — an ultimate — plan in mind for humankind.

Diane Tessman of Poway, Calif. has been in contact with ETs since an early age when she climbed aboard their ship while a child living in Iowa. Her repeated contacts and subsequent channelings from Tibus a Space Brother have been verified by the likes of Dr. Leo Sprinkle of the University of Wyoming, and Ruth Montgomery who writes about Diane in her best selling ALIENS AMONG US.

Following her lifelong contacts with these beings (leading up to the formation of her own STARLITE MYSTIC CENTER and the publication of THE TRANSFORMATION — CHANNELINGS

FROM TIBUS), Diane feels she is in an excellent position to theorize about the arrival of aliens on our world, thus offering the following seven points for debate:

Diane Tessman

1. One of the most popular theories is that some humans will be
saved when nuclear disaster strikes. The world is on the brink of
destruction with wars and crises springing up globally; one misguided leader with a nervous finger could push the nuclear button! If
we humans knew that a forest were to be bulldozed, would not some
of us responsibly rescue all the animals we could and move them
to a safe new environment? However, first we might make visits
to the forest and attempt to "make friends" with the animals so
that the trauma of change would not be too much for them. After
all, if the animal being saved dies of fright upon contact with its
rescuer, not much good is accomplished.

2. A variation on the nuclear disaster theme is the planetary natural disaster. Perhaps the world will shift on its axis, perhaps planetary alignment will pull Earth out of orbit, perhaps volcanic erupt-

ions or earthquakes will cause global flooding and fires and widespread disasters. This catastrophe should be predictable through the advanced technology which UFO occupants obviously possess and, again, a contact period with the individuals who are to be saved would be necessary before disaster strikes.

3. As Dr. Leo Sprinkle puts it, maybe UFO occupants are accustomed to us being UFO occupants. This idea can work in easily with theories One and Two also. If catastrophe does occur, it cannot be expected that rescued humans will be served in luxury by the UFO occupants forever. We would be expected in a sense to earn our way. They will need to educate us to be the crew of the starships and to work side by side with them, expanding our capacities for technical knowledge and for decency; in short, perhaps they can raise our intelligence to such a point that we will become them, for all intents and purposes. This would explain the shared identity which some abductees feel with individual crew members aboard UFOs. The identity would be vital to future successful functioning onboard the UFO.

4. Humans might be removed when the time is "right" to colonies, distant planets or space stations. This theory is similar to the idea of "us" becoming "them" onboard UFOs, but it also infers that the "chosen" people in the new colony originating from Earth might be Adams' and Eves', starting a new human race on a distant world, with the help of UFO friends.

5. Or perhaps the ultimate plan is to have abductees and contactees "infiltrate" modern Earth society with their enlightened messages of peace and the beauty of infinite diversity; humans who have had contact do seem to "become" aliens on their own world, seeing reality more clearly in cosmic terms.

6. Our theories thus far have been of the "nuts and bolts", variety. If we assume, however, that UFOs can also be from other dimensions then we might surmise that some UFOs could be pure spirit, and that abductees will be asked to join the occupants at a later date, after bodily "death." The British publication, FLYING SAUCER REVIEW, reports the case of a UFO landing and a "regular human" emerging from the ship. The witness talked to the

person who came out of the craft and was told the human's name. After checking, it was discovered that this person had been a "UFO buff," but had recently drowned! Apparently "death" was transitory because the man was now a crew member of a UFO. Was the "drowned" man saved right before death by UFO occupants and only presumed dead? Or, was he indeed dead in our terms, traveling aboard a soul/spirit ship which was encountered in this reality?

If Earth is to enter the galactic community, despite wars, starvation, pollution, and other serious problems, then there must be a driving energy from some humans who feel we simply must go into space. A few humans must be compelled, must feel the overpowering urge to travel the stars, otherwise, we will languish in the hole in which we now find ourselves. Perhaps the trait of needing to explore new horizons — of needing to reach for the stars — and the feeling that the stars are calling us home, can be implanted into the electrical currents that compose the mind. This "mind" might be passed along from one physical body to another, as time goes on through reincarnation. If a person has experienced a UFO abduction which has changed their entire outlook on life and the universe, then that great evolution might be impressed in the mind/soul, for future use in the next life. By the 25th Century, human minds, souls, and bodies may be traveling the galaxy. Will the seeds of this accomplishment have been started in 20th Century UFO abductions which opened minds and souls to the reality of other worlds?

QUESTIONS OF CONCERN

Over the years since she first released this information, Diane has been besieged with requests for additional data on the "lift-off" of humans from this planet. Recently, I sat down with her and held a brief interview with her on this very topic.

Beckley: One of the questions which keeps cropping up, when people write to me, is whether animals will be taken off the planet in the event of a global evacuation.

Diane Tessman: Tibus has given me the information that they very definitely will be taken. As a matter of fact, they have been taken in a planned scientific manner. There has been a Noah's Ark kind of thing going on for many years. Not only two of everything has been taken, but as many as possible to be seeded on new planets. These are planets which are hospitable as far as environment, but whose ecology would not be ruined by the introduction of earth life forms.

There are also huge space cities or even space countries orbiting outside our atmosphere, that are artificially created environments for life-forms from planets whose evacuation is imperative. This would include not just cows and horses, but also smallest insects and plants. Everything has been taken many times aboard the small shuttles, which people have been calling saucers, since 1947.

People who will be evacuated will be allowed to take pets, because it is considered necessary to their adjustment. They will also take family members, since they will take as many regular humans as possible. And if the family is with the star child, why wouldn't they be taken. The family is right there and the star child functions better with them. So there will be family members taken who are not star children, as well as pets, if this is something that the star child needs to function for the very important mission ahead.

Beckley: Another important question which keeps coming up is as to the number of people that will be taken. There seems to be a discrepancy among the various space channels on this, to the exact number of people that will be taken along, in case of an evacuation. Has Tibus ever given you any specific numbers?

Diane Tessman: He has assured me that as many will be taken as possible. As I have said, they have huge space cities, space countries, and even rural areas, small planets that are spaceships. He has also assured me that each star person and their family will have an abode area to live in, which will be much bigger than a cabin. It will be essentially a house, only within the mothership quarters.

Beckley: How long will be required to stay in those quarters?

Diane Tessman: Different star children have different missions. Some people will stay on board at their own choosing and become crew members, as Dr. Sprinkle says, "Us-folk will become U-folk."

Other people will herald the New Age on earth after earth has been cleansed of the radiation by the Space Brothers' advanced technology. Other star children will, by their own choice, seed new planets. This is the Adam and Eve syndrome.

Beckley: One of the things that has been told to us by the Space Brothers, is that the star children and walk-ins will be developing specific extraordinary abilities, which may not yet be known.

Diane Tessman: Among my star people, from the Network, I have some who are very dynamic healers and they feel that their energies are getting greater. Tibus has told me that there will be virtual "mash" units, which will require the star person healers' attention on any number of people with radiation burns and other injuries.

I have also been given the information that there are many star people who are emotional healers. This is more than comforting ability. This is an actual healing ability but of the mind. There will be many regular people who will be totally traumatized from seeing the destruction of the planet. They will have lost loved ones. They will have been injured, or have radiation burns, and suddenly they'll find themselves aboard a spaceship, and aliens — as they call the Space Brothers — will be attempting to heal them. The Space Brothers have both advanced scientific, and medical techniques, and also great healing abilities. The star person healers will be the bridge between the aliens and the regular humans. The ones who have the emotional healing ability will be able to soothe them. This will save people from going into shock and help them accept what has happened.

I have also been told that the star people are the adapters. They adapt energy. They operate on a higher level of energy and adapt it to the mundane level. They can also explain what is happening to the Space Brothers, who may have trouble understanding some human behavior. The Space Brothers can learn this psychically. But the star people are just invaluable interpreters and bridges between the two levels of consciousness.

There are other abilities which can be found within our star peoples' Network, besides healing. We have teachers, who often feel that they are to be the teachers of other teachers. They would work to expand the awareness of groups that are not quite as aware, once the New Age begins. They would acquaint people with the terms and the concepts which are needed to live in the New Age. We have other star people who have great artistic ability, who can channel as they paint or compose. We have quite a few musicians and composers. We have people who are experts in crystals. I have one gentleman who was given the idea, by the Space Brothers, that if crystals are cut in triangular shapes to the exact dimension of the great pyramids, they will give off more power. He was also given the Federations' flag in his channeling.

We also have people among us who are animal experts. They can heal animals and would like to work with the animals who are beamed up. So, we have those people who will be spending a lifetime as forest rangers, park rangers, and zoologists.

Our Star Network includes people with many different talents, from all walks of life. We have Muslims, we have those who believe in nature worship, we have many Christians. I feel, we are all striving towards Christ consciousness, though not all of us are within the realm of organized religion. I have not found one star person who does not believe in God, as the creative energy, as the life force in all of us and as the universal cosmic force. That seems to be another common denominator.

ARTEMIS SPEAKS

The following was channeled by Anthony Volpe, over a period of 45 minutes. It started as a mental communication with Lynn Volpe asking pertinent questions. Somewhere during the communication, Artemis chose to channel directly through Anthony. You will have to be the judge as to where the direct channeling began. A space being from a highly advanced culture, Artemis has spoken with the Pennsylvania couple many times.

June 21, 1981 10:00 P.M. to 10:45 P.M.

Q. "Can you see him?"

A. "Yes, his collar is like a nehru jacket. His jacket is a metallic silvery blue in color."

Q. "What is his mission?"

A. "He goes to other planets to help them from making the same mistake his planet did. He is now part of a team to assist in raising the vibrations of any planet in trouble."

Q. "How many are on his team?"

A. "There are 13,000 beings on his team."

Q. "What planet is he from?"

A. "Miranda, in an uncharted part of our galaxy".

Q. "Where are they now?"

A. "Their home base is a "Space Platform"; that is, a docking orbit around the earth. They project down spiritual energies to people of their sector of earth. Other craft like theirs also encircle earth."

Q. "What is their sector?"

A. "Their sector includes North America, part of Canada, and part of Mexico."

Q. "What part is Artemis to play in the evacuation?"

A. "They are assisting, but not taking people up. They will identify those who are to be taken. Another group will come in, and pickup the "chosen ones".

Q. "How many groups are involved in the evacuation?"

A. "There are many facets to the evacuation. Each facet has its own tier of responsibility with its own space craft."

Q. "List the facets, please."

A. "The Artemis group is in charge of aiding mankind in the lifting of their vibrations, and to thereby lessen the severity of the effects of the cataclysms. There are groups above that on "standby", that will be called upon to pick up those chosen by the Artemis group. There is a third group that will house the people brought up to their craft. They will be separated into groups according to their spiritual development. The groups must work with each other to help the space people to help those who are left behind. Not all of the chosen ones will be taken. The chosen who will remain here are beamed with energies to interest them in studying survival, natural medicine, psychic and spiritual healing. Many of the New Age workers and instructors who feel that they will be taken will not be taken right away, but left behind to help mankind survive through the cataclysmic period. This is their mission. Those left behind will be doing the jobs they have been trained for; then after a time, they will be taken. They will be augmented by those in the craft who have undergone training in spiritual upliftment of mankind. As future teachers, they will be sent back to save an additional number of people on earth. To awaken that spark that has been put within them, and to awaken that spark of spiritual awareness, so their growth will be rapid. Others remaining on the craft will receive them as a "welcoming committee" and as teachers to aid them in their spiritual development.

Earth people cannot leave the earth unless that individual is harmless if taken to a more highly evolved planet in the galaxy. A high degree of spirituality is required. Truly loving one another, and understanding one another, and to be ready to fulfill the needs of each other — an unselfish loving. In the event of a cataclysm, not all those left behind will perish, although many will perish. Those who refuse to be enlightened and infused with the light of God will be taken to other planets that are uninhabited, but habitable, and there they will make a new start.

All of this has been spoken of before! Know that it is true. It will happen. Believe in the prophets that are warning of the dire consequences that you can look forward to if you don't change what is in your heart, and your way of thinking. Cease the hatred which is many times masked so that the inner feelings do not show. That which is revealed is not always what is within.

The *inner* man must be changed and purged of greed, avarice, hatred, aggressiveness, as well as other loathsome adjectives that describe the inner nature of man in his present stage of evolution. Only after purging and infusion of *His* light can we expect to lessen, if not avert the cataclysms. But this does not seem likely, even though man has been warned for many years. Those few who have taken up the light are working at great odds trying to lift the vibrations of earth. Man does not realize that the combined thought of all mankind controls the nature of earth. When all is peace and harmony the earth will be peace and harmony. War and anger is that reflection of mankind that is coming back to him through the upheavals of natural disasters.

You see my friends, earth is a reflection of the inhabitants and not the other way around. We are here — be aware — we are here to help in many ways; however, the help is just that — help. We cannot do it for you. *It must come from within."*

Q. "Will the evacuation come soon?"

A. "Sooner than most people think, if the world continues in the violent condition that it presently is going through. The time cannot be set. The peace workers and brothers of the light will make themselves known by spreading their influence among others. The rapidity of the spread of goodness will delay the cataclysms, but they *will* come. The longer they are delayed, the more will be saved."

Q. "Will many be saved?"

A. "Yes, many will be saved."

Q. "Will this be a "physical" evacuation?"

A. "Yes, this will be a physical evacuation. Many people can consider themselves evacuated already because as they sleep, their bodies are amongst us.

The spreaders of peace and brotherhood throughout the world are not limited to one country, nation or continent around your globe. Some learn easier than others. Others, because of their religious dogmas and political philosophy are lagging behind, but we are making inroads in this area also."

Q. "What can Anthony and I do that we are not doing?"

A. "You are amongst the light workers. We have been in contact, and impressed upon you the importance of "preaching", if you will, through your various means of communication with people and groups, the facts as outlined to you and urging your fellow man and woman to love each other in a truly unselfish way. Not only to speak of brotherhood, but to practice it. For how can you love us as we love you if you cannot first love yourselves.

It must be made perfectly clear that we know exactly what is in the hearts of each and every person in our sector. Those that speak of love and brotherhood but are intolerant of their own people because of race, national or religious differences, those with these attitudes cannot hide behind lecturing upon platforms, or writing in magazines about love and brotherhood because *we know what is in their heart.*

Chicago-based psychic Irene Hughes says many incredible earth changes will take place and some of the Hawaiian Islands may even disappear.

Spiritual teacher Phillel of Mark Age, shown here standing in front of the Apollo Moon Module, says that many of the inhabitants of this planet will soon by moving upward into the fourth dimension.

This warning is not for you sister Lynn or brother Anthony, but those who hear this warning will know if it applies to them. In answer to your question, do what you have been doing. But *Do it more vigorously.* Reach out to as many people as you can. Use the spoken word, and the mental word. Pray for the enlightenment of those whom you know should know better. Your thoughts and prayers are heard in other realms and relayed to those people on earth that you are praying for to help awaken them to their God self which lies within."

Q. "Will we have a nuclear war?"

A. "We are trying our best to prevent that. If it does happen, it will be through man's own stupidity."

Q. "What is the name or number of your ship?"

A. "We do have a number but it would be meaningless to you because it is not of your numeric system, and would be foreign to any of those presently in use on your planet. It is a universal system which is used by all of the higher order of beings, those that are permitted space travel."

Q. "Could we have a physical meeting with one of your kind?"

A. "This is the last question for this evening. It is very difficult indeed for one of us to come down to your planet for the purpose of your seeing us in the physical form. We see no need for this. Do you doubt our existence? If you do, it would be meaningless to make ourselves visible. If you do not doubt then it would not be necessary. Much time and preparation is required for one of our kind to leave our craft and come down to *socialize.* Be certain the work we are doing is better served right where we are now."

I go now and I leave you both with my blessings and my encouragement to keep on with your good work. Until we speak again, may you both be bathed in *His* light."

Artemis

Lynn and Anthony willingly theorize about Artemis' message thusly:

"No doubt there is a stern warning in Artemis' message, but also

— 72 —

a message of hope.

"The term 'chosen ones' should be obvious that this is necessitated by ones past karma; in other words, we choose ourselves. *It must be earned.* The space ships are craft of a harmonious vibration. If one of a very negative auric field were to be taken along with those "chosen" this would create dischord, besides the person who is not ready could not withstand the high frequency vibration that he would encounter. 'Many are called and few are chosen' means 'many are called and few choose to listen'. No one is being excluded purposely. We are not saying this one stays and this one goes, per se. It is a matter of harmonious loving vibrations. It will be nobody's fault if many remain behind. Certainly not the fault of our Space Brothers and Sisters. We know the path. It has been outlined for us many times before. All mankind has to do now is change from within and develop a sense of love for self and others, and then he may be taken. But nothing will be given to those who by their negativity refuse the opportunity. For those who feel upset with these messages, this is the time to lock within oneself for possible correction — as we all need to do this at times. But it is very easy to show a state of "emotional love" to others, and say "I love you, I love you" to someone's face, and then the minute the back is turned, become knit picky and gossipy about speakers, neighbors, loved ones, etc . . . true love is not emotionalism. It is quiet gentle caring for others *behind their backs,* coupled with loving thoughts and a desire for the growth and development of others without jealousy. Give a word of encouragement to somebody and surely you'll be amongst those who have 'chosen' themselves for the evacuation."

WHEN ON EARTH WILL THE SPACESHIPS LAND?

When on earth will the spaceships land? When will the mass landings, the official contacts, the concrete proofs occur that we've all been waiting and praying for these many years? When on earth *will* the spaceships land? Phillel of the Florida based New Age group called Mark Age has a few finely tuned ideas which take into consideration the thousands of pages of material which their leader Yolanda has channeled over the course of several decades. As the following data from this source indicates, they are expecting the spaceships to land openly fairly soon, as they say Earth continues to expand its cosmic awareness and gets itself ready for some *big* changes.

* * *

Since the very beginning of the spiritual space program in 1960, the space brothers of the Federation of Planets of our solar system have maneuvered themselves for official, mass landings of their craft on earth. Specifically, attempts to land were made in 1961, 1963 and 1966. Also in 1968 they communicated through Nada-Yolanda, primary channel of Mark-Age, that they were holding to the ideal that landings would occur no later than 1972.

But now we are nearly through the 1980s and still are awaiting fulfillment of these plans. So, where do we stand? What can we expect?

To answer these questions, let's define first what we mean by mass landings. Mass landings do not necessarily mean the landing of massive numbers of spacecraft. Rather, they *can* mean the selective, possibly simultaneous landings of a few ships that will be witnessed or known about by mass numbers of people.

Granted, thousands of landings have occurred on our planet since the beginning of the modern UFO era almost four decades ago. But what we're discussing here are those encounters that will bring undeniable, irrefutable, concrete evidence to the world at large that we have now established official contact with visitors from other planets.

Let's remind ourselves here of some of the principles involved in mass landings. Because of the evolved spiritual consciousness of our visitors, they are bound by cosmic law not to interfere with or to override man's free will. Therefore, landings can only occur when man's consciousness has been raised to accept these events and all the dramatic changes that will result on a planetary scale.

But man's receptivity is the only thing involved. He must also be spiritually prepared to handle the higher vibrational frequencies that the space visitors bring with them by the very nature of their materialized forms. You see, in order to land, the visitors have to transmute or lower their frequency vibration into our third dimensional level, to appear solid. This applies not only to those beings who express on a fourth dimensional, etheric level but also to those who express on physical vibrations that yet are more refined than our own.

So, a certain meshing or merging of our two vibrational levels has to be expertly synchronized before lasting contact can be made. This means that as they lower their vibration to make contact, we simultaneously must raise our vibration — psychically, physically and otherwise — to interlock with their level. Sounds pretty complicated, doesn't it?

Here's the way Dr. Hannibal, an etheric space commander, put it in a channeling through Yolanda on January 3, 1969: "We cannot allow you to have much contact with our solidified form until you have been raised sufficiently to satisfy your concepts and your own body forms without destroying them or damaging them to a degree that would be irreparable... We will not do this until you are ready to be able to indulge in the higher rates of frequency that we shall bring with us by the nature of our being."

This brings us back to mass landings. The fact that they haven't occurred fully yet means that up to this point we have been able to handle only so much direct contact with their forms. Of course, this is evolving and changing all the time as the mass spiritual awakening on the planet unfolds.

MASS EDUCATIONAL PLAN

A great part of this spiritual awakening comes through educating the masses to the realities of spiritual life in our universe. And even though mass landings have remained as a plan in the works all these years, what has been stressed equally is the need to educate and to prepare mankind spiritually.

Actually, the space visitors in the early 1960's outlined in advance just how their program generally would proceed, regarding mass sightings, landings, contacts and education. Their predictions have proven out. Listen to these excerpts. The first two were channeled through Yolanda, and the second two were channeled through Gloria Lee.

On September 11, 1960, a space brother named Euell said this about landings: "There may be a few isolated cases, where we feel friendly reception will take place, that there will be face-to-face communication."

On November 14, 1960, Wains stated: "You will have some physical contact during the mass sightings, those who are ready for such; but it will not be on a large scale. It will be very selective. When the full educational program is completed...we can walk among you as equals and help you to overcome the false concepts of your world."

On December 14, 1960, J.W. channeled: "Much educating of the planet would be done before any mass landings would take place... When this has been done and the people understand the reasons and the causes of why we are here...then will they be given opportunity to view our ships by our landing and placing ourselves at your disposal...Until we can focus the love vibration and can use every possible means at our disposal to help in the educational program of the planet, we will not create mass demonstrations until we have seen whether or not this will be successful."

Again, on Decembr 19, 1960, J.W. said, "We are working in the etheric realm...to fulfill a great educational progam that will bring attention of us to the public in general. As this program is being developed there will be more sightings through various parts of the planet. This in a sense will be to back up what is given in the educational program...

"All these things will manifest right along with the educational program. So even though there are not the mass sightings as you have anticipated, there will be other forms of diversion which will take place in your skies both day and night for the whole planet to view and to understand."

There you have it. From the early days, the space brothers revealed how they would coordinate landing attempts with a planetary educational program. And this is exactly what has happened. These promises have been fulfilled: 1) We have continued to have mass sightings. (2) Selective, isolated landings, involving close encounters of the second and third kind, have occurred. 3) The masses have been conditioned by a literal barrage of educational materials on space visitors, ranging from scientific investigative periodicals to popular books and magazines to positive films like "Close Encounters" and "E.T." Millions of people worldwide have been exposed to reports and experiences of contact with extraterrestrials. All this has been part of preparing man for eventual contact with his brothers and sisters of the cosmos.

ON THE THRESHOLD OF CONTACT

Let's jump a step further. From 1972 to 1984, the spiritual plan was in a phase known as the mass educational program. This was one of three major cycles of this transitional period from 1960 to 2000 A.D. In 1984, the mass educational phase was completed, and the Hierarchy announced that we had entered the third and last cycle, known as the demonstration phase. This is where we stand now.

The light workers throughout the planet are beginning a new level of demonstrating Christ consciousness. This involves new manifestations of our resurrected, fourth dimensional form, known as the light body. Yes, the veil between dimensions, *is* thinning rapidly, and the spiritual program has entered an entirely new octave. As was stated in the popular movie "2010," "Something wonderful is going to happen!"

In late 1981, Dr. Hannibal, etheric commander for space activities and manifestations in the Western hemisphere, revealed to Yolanda that during the transmutation cycle we are in now — which has been dubbed the rending of the sixth phase of the seventh, and which lasts from 1982 through 1988-92 — we would have more direct proof of and contact with visitors from other planets.

It is now 1985. Are you beginning to understand what this means? That's right. *We are on the verge of contact that will give man of earth incontrovertible evidence to life in our solar system and be-*

yond. Though momentarily poised on this threshold, soon we are to be born into our cosmic citizenship amongst the stars!

The vibration of the planet and life forms on it is being raised to make this connection. The image that comes to my mind is that of two beings reaching out to one another, their arms stretched to the limit, their hands piercing inch by inch the misty veil that separates them. Their fingers, quivering with the strain of extension, move ever nearer, slowly closing the narrow gap. Now, in a burst of heroic effort, they are about to touch, to glide smoothly into contact, finally to clasp.

So, my friends *when* on earth will the space-ships land? Today? This year? Next year? This decade? Since we are on the threshold of a cosmic event, the answer is: soon! Only Spirit knows the day, the hour, the moment; for only Spirit knows the precise timing of this delicate synchronization.

So, in our meditations let's grasp that arm extended to us from outer space and higher dimensions. With love welling up within us, transforming us, raising us, let us move ourselves to merge with our space brothers and sisters. This love, this desire, this thought will help raise the entire planetary force field. Yes, my dear brothers and sisters of planet earth, the contact and reunion we yearn for is — how shall we say it? — *strictly inevitable!*

* * *

Certainly Phillel's opinions can only be considered his own, but in light of the seemingly legitimate material that has continued to be channeled by Yolanda of Mark Age for many years it might be wise to consider the words of wisdom they offer. Indeed, before mass landings can transpire Mark Age maintains a rigid schedule has been laid out for Earth's advancement by the Ashtar Command and the Federation of Planets. Mark Age outlines this many fold plan accordingly.

SITE PREPARATIONS

Through the channelings of Nada-Yolanda, the Hierarchy has outlined the following key preparations for landing operations.

TIME & SHIPS. It takes months and years for the Ashtar Command to adequately prepare landing sites and individuals for contact. Also, in landing operations, thousands of ships are involved, not just the one or several that materialize physically.

These invisible craft step down the vibrations of the landing ships in a gradual, step-by-step order. The step-down may take several days, to allow both the spaceships and the Earth population to absorb the vibrational frequency level and to adjust to the maneuver; preparations on both sides must mesh simultaneously.

In one possible scenario, several ships could land concurrently in different areas of the world, since multiple landing sites may be involved. In some instances, rather than descend from the skies, spaceships simply may materialize on their landing spots.

Generally speaking, light workers whose physical participation would be requested for a landing need not worry about being notified as to time and place of demonstration. The space brothers have means to give adequate signals, even simultaneously, to channels or others who need instructions.

INTERDIMENSIONAL TRAVEL. Spaceships coming from etheric planes first must travel or lower their vibrational frequency through the astral planes of Earth in order to manifest on the physical plane. So, astral forces have to be prepared in order to secure the physical landing area. For example, one instance recorded in "Visitors From Other Planets" shows where the space visitors negotiated with Indian astral forces for uses and rights of certain areas around a landing site.

Even craft manifesting from higher physical dimensions must be coordinated with astral levels at landing sites, because vibrational influences affecting one plane also are imprinted on the other.

CLEARING OF ATMOSPHERE. Both the mental and the physical atmospheres have to be tested, screened and cleansed of undesirable conditions before spacecraft can manifest. Scout ships, which are under supervision of larger craft housing speicalized equipment, help test specific areas.

Higher command ships may relay orders daily to test the group consciousness, as situations on Earth can change quickly due to man's freewill actions. Delays, misappropriations, emergencies or catastrophes can interfere with obtaining clearance to land. In addition, certain atmospheric conditions have to be taken into consideration only at the time of demonstration. For these reasons, it is difficult for the Ashtar Command to predict the exact time, location and nature of a spacecraft materialization or landing.

CLEARING OF CONTACTEE. Any person involved in a physical landing must be cleansed and cleared both by his inner plane guides and teachers and by his own high Self; everything must check out satisfactorily beforehand. Whether or not the contactee is aware of it, he has been prepared for contact through mental and physical conditionings. Other persons in the area, such as business or government officials who may be required to follow through, also must be cleansed enough to allow the higher force to penetrate.

Individuals might react adversely, however, to inner plane preparations and thus cancel out their key participation. Anytime individuals are involved, free will is involved; so any number of complications or problems could set in and cause alterations in the landing plan, even at the last stages of preparation.

LAND & LOWER KINGDOMS. Animal, vegetable and mineral kingdoms, as well as devic and elemental forces, have to be prepred.. The land (physical ground) must be cleared magnetically, and its vibration raised, so as to hold the higher force field of a spacecraft that can materialize and dematerialize at will. The special preparation of the land is to prevent permanent radiation damage due to the higher frequency vibrations; which, after all, must be injected into Earth in order to raise it.

Minimal damage still occurs at times. Evidence shows that in some UFO landing-trace cases, where the ground is burned or desiccated, after effects on ground and vegetation can remain for a long time.

SUITABLE AREAS. Certain areas are more suitable for landings. The space visitors have said, for instance, that it is easier for them to make contacts at high altitudes than at lower altitudes. In part, accessibility has to do with magnetic lines of force (extraterrestrial spacecraft, for their propulsion, operate on magnetic wave currents, which are different around each planet). But a clear or clean environment and a rarified atmosphere also are desirable. The Southwest in the United States, for example, has been tagged as one important focal point for contact.

Of course, space sightings and landings have occurred all over the world, in all types of environments and altitudes, and have involved people of all ages and walks of life.

PERMISSION NOT GRANTED ON PHYSICAL. Our space brothers and sisters have informed us that, because of the above considerations, permission to use specific landing sites is not something we can grant on the physical level.

ALTERNATE PLANS. Throughout these complex preparations, where so much may be altered through man's adverse reactons to contact, the space visitors maintain quintessential poise. On September 17, 1961, Dr. Hannibal channeled: "Our way of life and thinking is so much more advanced than yours, our level of comprehension and coordination and union of forces is so great that should all orders be cancelled in a split second of cancelling-out those instructions which have taken years of planning and plotting, no one would question or regret."

PHYSICAL PICKUP

Perhaps the most exciting prospect of Operation Landing Light is our potential participation in face-to-face contact and communication with space beings. Ufologists dub such experiences "close encounters of the third kind." Referring to cases where the contactee is allowed to board the craft, possibly even to go for a ride within the Earth's atmosphere, the space brothers prefer the term "pickup." Pickup also refers to being picked up, or raised, in consciousness. Following are a few keys for understanding space pickup.

LOVE. As emphasized repeatedly, love is the great motivating force behind all actions of our space visitors. Adhering to the spiritual law of love is their prime directive. In these Latter Days, the visitors never intentionally have harmed anyone on Earth. In the early 1960s, the Hierarchal Board instituted special protective measures to safeguard all space contacts with us. Therefore, all spaceships that enter our atmosphere are informed about and are part of the hierarchal program.

HIGH SELF PERMISSION. Ultimate permission for physical pickup is given by the contactee's high Self and by his or her inner plane teachers. In spite of the many conditionings he or she undergoes to be cleared, the individual may not necessarily acknowledge this permission consciously.

Some contactees, having incarnated from other planes or planets, actually have made preincarnational agreements to be picked up by their former associates, so as to help establish new patterns of interdimensional contact between the Federation and Earth. Again, the person may not be aware consciously of this agreement, though the high Self is aware and is fully cooperative.

The space visitors coordinate with our high Self and our teachers, and thus do not override anyone's free will as a child of God. There are some people, who judge with mortal consciousness, who consider physical pickups to be intrusions or violations. This judgment is false. Our space brothers do not force their contact on anyone.

COSMIC LAW. On August 30, 1961, during preparations for the first mass landing attempt, Tukari channeled: "When we land we will invite some to board our craft. We retain the right and the privilege to do this. We have the means to enforce this right. In no manner or means does this portray hostility, for we do not use any form of arms, as you recognize them, for destruction. We do have self-defense and protection in case of disorderly conduct."

The right and the privilege Tukari speaks of involves the cosmic law of give-and-take. Given the amount of time, energy and interdimensional coordination involved, the space brothers, once materialized and given clearance, are within their spiritual right to follow through with the planned pickup. This does not violate our free will, because from the high Self consciousness we freely and lovingly have agreed to cooperate.

The space brothers do not take us on board without giving us something in return. Through their love, protection and concern, which are continued after the contact, we receive spiritual support. Consequently, many contactees report spiritual transformations of their lives. Many awaken to cosmic awareness, to psychic talents, and to greater service of mankind.

FREQUENCY SHIFTS. Contact with beings of higher dimensions challenges us to elevate our third dimensional vibration; to meet them halfway, so to speak. The more we prepare ourselves spiritually, the better able we are to handle the vibrational frequency shift inherent to physical encounters. As light workers, one of our goals is to demonstrate, in I Am consciousness, the preeminent poise by which all contactees eventually will exchange with extraterrestrials.

The space visitors exercise extra special care in interacting with our life forms, so as not to short-circuit our normal physical and mental functions. Although risks have been minimized, physical contact with highly charged fourth dimensional vibrations may produce temporary misalignment or discombobulation of our four lower bodies. This occurs because our bodies are being raised into synchronization with the higher energies of the spacecraft, the occupants and our own light body.

Temporary reactions commonly experienced by contactees during physical pickup include altered states of consciousness, trance, involuntary out-of-body (astral) travel, mental disorientation, emotional upset, even partial amnesia ("missing time"). During or after contact, temporary physical reactions to higher vibratory frequencies include nausea, dizziness, headaches, numbing or tingling sensations, immobility, drowsiness or greater need for sleep, and skin and eye irritations.

Other, more positive reactions also may result, such as instantaneous healing, spiritual upliftment, cosmic realization, euphoria and rapture.

Mental and emotional reactions, which oftentimes are traumatic to the spiritually uninitiated, leave powerful imprints on the subconscious of the contactee. Therefore, memories that many have recalled, especially through means of hypnotic regression, have been badly distorted, misrepresented or misinterpreted. Fears, biases, preconceptions and runaway imagination (fantasy) all can color unintentionally the individual's recollections.

As a technique, hypnosis can be suspect, for controlled scientific studies have shown that false memories can be invented or "recalled" during hypnosis. In addition, many times the mental and emotional biases of the hypnotist or the investigator are projected, consciously or unconsciously, onto the highly suggestible subject.

Because of this potential discoloration by contactee and investigator alike, obtaining accurate recall in many cases becomes almost impossible. Hence, we advise all to use extreme caution in accepting information obtained through hypnosis. Exercise your spiritual discernment just as you would in evaluating channeled communications.

If hypnosis must be employed — and sometimes it has been useful to help the person mentally and emotionally integrate his or her experience — it should be performed under strictly supervised conditions by an expertly qualified physician or psychologist. Care should be taken to eliminate emotional bias and all possible leading questions.

MEDICAL EXAMINATIONS. It is apparent, through reports of cases others have investigated, that the space visitors perform physical examinations on many whom they pick up.

As revealed in channelings through Yolanda, the space brothers have ultra-sophisticated technology. For example, with their equipment (and often with their psychic powers) they can read a person's aura, or subtle energy fields of the physical and the invisible bodies. They can read thought patterns. They can diagnose deficiencies or areas that need healing. With computerlike hieronic equipment on board certain etheric ships, they can chart our progress, as individuals and as a race, in the transmutation from third into fourth dimension.

Although we have received no communications regarding on-board physical examinations, it is likely the space visitors perform them not to satisfy mere curiosity but to test our health and the reactions of our astral, mental, emotional and physical bodies to contact with their higher vibrations. Through these tests, they may help determine our status in the dimensional changeover.

Examination of the physical body possibly includes observation of our atomic/molecular/genetic structure. But claims of sexual intercourse, fertilizations, abortions and hybridizations are not tenable. Lastly, reports of alleged physical implants in contactees probly are misperceptions, either psychic or physical, or examination techniques; no physical evidence has been produced.

APPROACHING A CRAFT. If you see a landed spacecraft, act with common sense. Do not approach and/or touch the craft until you are informed it is safe to do so, for it may emit higher frequency vibrations deleterious to your third dimensional body. Some people, acting too quickly, accidentally have been burned or otherwise injured. The space brothers take all precautions possible to prevent accidental exposure.

Above all, remain calm. Have no fear. Greet the visitors with love and brotherhood. For in that light they land.

We shall be tapping into Mark Age's many spiritual ''sources'' throughout the pages of this book.

CHAPTER SIX

The Ashtar Command And Operation Landing Light

His words have been received by many the world over. And while no one has ever seen him in a physical sense, few can deny that he speaks with a power and a majesty that heralds great wisdom and knowledge that could only have been obtained through centuries of deep study and enlightenment. There are those who steadfastly maintain that Ashtar is about the wisest space being assigned to our solar system, a dedicated and highly advanced soul who has reincarnated many times to the point where he can now truly be considered a Master in the same category as Jesus, Buddha and other avatars. In short he is the Messenger of the New Age, assigned to the task of bringing Earth safely through the troubled times that will most certainly cross our path in the next few years.

One earthly channel who wishes to identify himself only by the initials E.P.H. has received many messages from Ashtar through automatic writing, as well as while in an altered state of consciousness. This channel makes the point that throughout both psychic phenomena and the Bible, "there are orders of beings, called by

various names, who in times of great need, especially, come to earth to offer their assistance to men. Why shouldn't they be able to impress thoughts and ideas on receptive individuals," E.P.H. justly wants to know. "After all," the channel reminds us, "down through the ages there have been mystics who claimed they have heard the voice of God or of angels. Today, there are those who claim to hear the voice of spacemen. And if flying saucers are real, why shouldn't they be manned by intelligent beings who can send their thought-waves to those who are receptive?" It would appear that Ashtar has been doing exactly what E.P.H. suggests, and the scope of his influence is expanding as more and more sensitive individuals are picking up on his words of encouragement.

GUARDIAN ACTION

Among those who claim to have channeled Ashtar is Thelma Terrell head of Guardian Action International, and an acknowledged New Age leader. Thelma says her calling as a spiritual messenger began in the early Seventies, with her channeling work starting in 1979, when she was commissioned by the Ashtar Command to use the spiritual name of "Tuella". Tuella has published *World Messages For The Coming Decade,* a cosmic symposium of some 27 speakers (including nine noted Space Commanders and representatives of the Saturnium Council, as well as the very popular book *Project World Evacuation.*

In recent transmissions which she has received via mental telepathy from the Ashtar Command, this highly evolved intelligence says that news of disasters will soon reach a magnitude that the news media will be at a loss to report them all. "Television reports will fill the day in continuing attempts to cover these events, so recurrent will be the disasters, so widespread the locations. These have been referred to as changes that must come. The restlessness of the inner earth which awakens the sleeping volcanoes to belch forth their living fire, is the same momentum which manifests elsewhere as tremors or earthquakes of small or large magnitude. Tidal waves and intense weather abnormalities; shifting plates of land beneath the oceans and the quivering of the mountains, could take place in concerted action, so that humanity would have nowhere to run, no where to turn and no sense of direction or idea of what they must do to save themselves. Panic could grip the hearts of people resulting in calls upon God for deliverance. It is in hours such as these THAT YOUR SKIES WILL FILL WITH THE SHIPS OF YOUR BROTHERS FROM OTHER REALMS."

One of the things that the Ashtar Command has requested at this point in time is that they be allowed to come forward and be permitted to take a place in the international body as well as in our own Congress.

"We extend to your President, the House of Representatives, the men of the Senate and all of the national leaders, our hand of friendship and cooperation. In the name of the salvation of the life of Humanity, we ask that you would receive our words and welcome us to speak in your assemblies. We have those who can walk among you and never be noticed for all their similarity to your own appearance. They can suddenly appear behind your rostrum and speak to the members of your Congress. We would prefer to be invited to do this. If we are not invited to do this we may have to arrange our own opportunity, to speak to these gentlemen, in the early part of this decade. For there is too much at stake on an interplanetary basis to stand by without an effort to probe the motivations behind present world disorder. We send this message as an advancing envoy and ask the world leaders and the governments of all the world to make a place for our spokesmen upon your agendas."

Ashtar's closing words on this matter is quite clear:

"IF THE SPACE IS MADE THE SPOKESMAN WILL APPEAR!"

Could it be that shortly our world leaders will have to start listening to these highly evolved beings, regardless of whether they want to or not?

Some time ago, I had the honor to share the same speakers platform in Reno, Nevada with Tuella and during a brief break in the proceedings managed to sneak in a casual interview with this remarkable New Age lady whose channeling abilities has reaped her a host of dedicated students from coast to coast. Here is what Tuella had to tell me about Ashtar, her version of the planned evacuation, and the overall plan of our brothers and sisters from the depths of space.

Beckley: You are one of the many channels who are in regular contact with Ashtar and his command. What sort of messages are now coming through?

Teulla: Most of the recent channeling have to do with a mass evacuation off this globe before a disaster strikes. My book PROJECT: WORLD EVACUATION was meant to help get people ready and to know what to expect. In this way much of the trauma is removed should that event become necessary.

Beckley: How did you first start channeling, what is your background in this field, and what were you doing before you got involved in all this?

Tuella: I was a servant of Jesus Christ long before I knew anything about this. I was a pastor, an evangelist and I was a lover of the scriptures. My first unusual experience came when I'd be seeking scriptures for my sermons. Someone would be standing behind me discussing certain passages. It began in that fashion — someone hovering over me and teaching me. Then, finally the things I was taught far exceeded the creed to which I was bound. Soon, I moved out and the teachings expanded. That is how I found a closer relationship with my own spiritual teachers.

Beckley: For those not so familiar with this sort of thing, could you tell us something about Ashtar, and the Ashtar Command, and those that make up his group?

Tuella: Ashtar himself is a very beautiful being. He is from the Venus heritage line. There are six planets up there, there is Venus, and Astara, Volga, and Ashtar, and Eros, and that group of planets. He is from that line, but he is the Commander in Chief of this hemisphere, for all the fleets that are coming in from all of the other planets and galaxies. We have other commanders who are in charge of other hemispheres. Ashtar has been called the Christian Commander and he is very close to the Lord Jesus Christ. Of course, Jesus is referred to as our great beloved Commander. The next in authority over Ashtar is Jesus Sananda Himself. All that takes place within the atmosphere of the earth is the responsibility of the space federation which is under the direct jurisdiction of Ashtar himself.

Beckley: You are a space channel. You do receive messages from Ashtar and from those under his command. Have you ever seen Ashtar materialize? Have you seen him in the physical sense, and could you describe him?

Tuella: He does not materialize. These fellows from this level of evolution do not materialize. What they do is send a projection of themselves to you, so that rather than seeing, you perceive. If you are sensitive, you sense what they look like and what they are wearing.

In the opening pages of my book, I do get into a description of what is was like when Ashtar appeared to me and I use the term "appear" loosely. When he appears, it is a projection that he sends, mind to mind, just as he sends his words mind to mind. It is truly a function of telepathy.

Beckley: How many messages have you channeled to date?

Tuella: I have no idea there have been so many. I still have in my files pretty much everything I have ever received. I have 12 years of training with them.

One of the beings very prominent in my training is a being called Athena. I did not know at the time anything about the Space Confederation, but I found out later that Athena is the twin flame of Ashtar. He has said to me that he could turn over the whole command to her and no one would even miss him. She is that efficient in her job. She is the one who had taken over my training for many years. It was not until 1980 that Ashtar came in and asked me to take over a certain chore, and began to communicate with me in a direct way. But, even now, he does not come in unless it is something of great importance. Usually, one of the other commanders or someone else comes in.

Beckley: What, at this moment, would you say is their most important function?

Tuella: The most important thing right now is that they want the world to know why they are here. They want fear removed so it will not hinder what they are trying to do. And they want the world to know that there is a very, very strong possibility that events may make a world evacuation necessary before much longer.

They have indicated that there probably will be great geological changes, not necessarily war. They do not intend to let nuclear war go on for any length of time. But, nuclear war may precipitate severe geological events.

Beckley: How many people have they chosen for this evacuation and how have they been chosen?

Tuella: They do not choose people for this evacuation. The people have already made their choices long ago. Therefore, they qualify by virtue of the lives they have lived, and by the frequency of their own electromagnetic field or their aura as it is called. If they had their way they would take everyone and everyone would go. Everyone will receive an invitation, but not everyone can endure the frequencies of the levitation beams.

ASHTAR'S END TIME NOTES

Needless to say, it is not within the scope of this present publication to document all the many messages that have been channeled from Ashtar and other members of the various federations of planets that are said to exist throughout the vast universe. For what could we offer in the way of proof that these disclosures are not the work of over-active imaginations? No scientific method is presently available to verify that which must for the present still be referred to as the supernatural or paranormal. We can only take each message or group of messages and test them out to our own satisfaction. When dealing with anything in the realm of the psychic it is always necessary to use a little of your own sensitivity to separate the wheat from the chaff.

Carol Rodriguez is a talented artist from Jackson Heights, New York, who has for quite a number of years remained actively interested in the subject of UFOs and in the possibility that human-like space beings are monitoring our activities down here on earth. Her mind has remained open to new ideas and thoughts which others might reject out of hand simply because they might at first seem far fetched. Carol knows that anything is possible as she has experienced any number of psychic related manifestations in her life which have enabled her to draw the conclusion that other entities co-exist along with mankind in the same solar system in which we reside.

Recently, Carol has been present when a dedicated young man was seen fit to serve as a "go between" for the Ashtar Command. This individual refused to allow his identity to be made public since he believes it would hamper his ongoing work. "He doesn't find it necessary to go before the public," Carol explains, "as he feels the notoriety would only take away from the importance of the message and would place him in the spotlight instead of the actual source for this information, which must now be gotten out to the public at all cost."

In addition to being the one who has had the privilege of asking questions of Ashtar, Carol has also been of tremendous help in transcribing the tapes of the dozen or more communications that have to date been beamed through this nameless channel.

And while the messages from Ashtar have covered a wide variety of topics, Ashtar seems most anxious to get his specific thoughts across on the very subject we are so fascinated by, mainly the End Times.

The following notes have been taken directly from the cassette tapes hereby known as the Ashtar End Time Notes. Some editing for clarity sake has been done, but the essence remains true to the actual discourses. We have decided to present the material in a series of questions, followed by, in most instances, a most relevant answer. And while there are still missing pieces of the puzzle that we will fill in later on, these messages, I feel, go a long way in adding to our knowledge of the Last Days.

WHEN WILL YOU LAND AND EVACUATE THE EARTH?

The time is not so far away. When that time *does* arrive, you and the other chosen ones will be taken up to a safe place in outer space. Perhaps this will be on some other planet, or a large mothership. From there you can watch your planet being destroyed. Should the end come through an explosion, a nuclear war (which we will do our best to prevent), we will monitor the radiation from space, and do the best we can to sweep your atmosphere clean so that those that have been chosen, and who have been taken up, can eventually be brought back to earth later on.

It is impossible to predict an exact date, however, things are leading up to a point where such an event cannot be postponed much longer. Your planet's vibrations are very, very negative. There are many forces on your planet that are seeking to control the destiny of millions and millions of people.

Things are bad. Things are disastrous. It could happen at any time. It could happen tomorrow. It could happen a week from now. It could happen a year from now, or five years from now. It is impossible to predict the exact date, but there are some things that will happen, some things that you can watch for and mark on your calendar.

WHAT ARE SOME OF THESE SIGNS YOU SPEAK OF?

There will be a country in the Middle East that will be overtaken by the country you call the Soviet Union. When this happens the time will not be far off. When this happens the time will be close at hand. Such is happening now in Afghanistan, but it will spread.

The power of the Soviet Union is very mighty. They are very powerful. They have a great military machine. Your United States feels that it is the will of the people that we try to liberate these people living under the Soviet Union and the Communist Manifesto. While it is certainly brave and courageous that your government feels this way, it is also leading you down the path to a nuclear holocaust.

The two forces are opposing. They are like magnets, magnets that repel each other, and this can only lead to a catastrophe. It is too bad that this has to happen. We would like to see it avoided, but it will be difficult to do so. You have built your military up to the point where both nations could, very easily, destroy themselves through a nuclear holocaust. There is no backing out now, it seems. Both countries are very influential in the world. The next war could possibly be a very disastrous one. Millions of people will be killed, millions of people will be slaughtered but some — the lucky ones — will be saved.

We will come. We will land. We will make ourselves known. We will take on board those who are worthy, those who are aware of our presence, those who are involved in the New Age.

IF THERE WERE A NUCLEAR HOLOCAUST, WOULDN'T THIS CAUSE PROBLEMS IN OUTER SPACE? WOULDN'T THE ENTIRE SOLAR SYSTEM BE AFFECTED?

Yes, this is true. You see, if there were a nuclear holocaust on your planet, it would cause a vibration like a chain reaction that would vibrate through the entire solar system and would cause negative effects. It might cause, not only a disturbance in your polar alignment, but it could also cause this to happen on several other planets. It is possible indeed and so we have to watch you with keen interest. Not only do we not want you to destroy yourselves, but we don't want to see any of our other brothers throughout the solar system destroyed either.

CAN'T YOU DO SOMETHING TO STOP THESE THINGS FROM HAPPENING?

We are doing what we can at this time. There are people amongst you who are from the various planets in the solar system and they are trying to get to your leaders, trying to get them to see the situation they are getting into. But it is really impossible to change the minds of individuals. Though we can alert them to the facts, though we can try to shine the light of universal love on them, it is impossible if their will is not strong enough to want to change. For you see there is not just one leader on your planet. Your own President for example, he does not have the power. The power is given to many. It is given to the scientist. It is given to the military. This is true not only in the United States, but also in other countries. Not one person holds the key to peace. If this were the case, we would probably come down and take him away and all would be well. It is true that some are willing to listen. Many others refuse to as it is their own greed that they are looking out for, not the welfare of their own people, or the welfare of space people throughout this solar system.

CAN YOU TELL US MORE ABOUT THE HOLOCAUST?

There will be a natural holocaust that will take place, caused, not only by the nuclear explosions of war, but because your own weather, your own atmosphere, is so rapidly changing. You have already seen this with the repeated eruptions of the volcano you call Mount St. Helens in Washington state, but there will be others that will be taking place around the world. There will be an increase in earthquakes and volcanic eruptions, and these will also cause many related disasters and loss of life. These are all signs the time is near, that times are changing, that your whole planet is going through a change.

We would like to see these things not happen as they would be bad for all of us. But it is impossible to change the course of history. We could look, we could observe, we could do what we can, but we can not change the facts.

You have created your own life, your own civilization, and it is impossible for us to come down and actually interfere. This would be against the universal laws. We might even be able to give you advice, but if you do not listen it is not up to us to prevent these things. This is a natural occurrence, something you have brought upon yourselves, and you will have to pay the karmic consequences.

There will be more signs in the heavens. Mankind will look to the stars for their salvation. All this will happen shortly. Within the next few years there will be many, many changes taking place on your planet. We are watching from far above, keeping tabs on your activities. We are hoping, we are praying, that these events do not transpire.

COULD ANY OF THIS STILL BE AVERTED? IS THERE A PRAYER FOR MANKIND?

Yes, there is a chance this can all be averted, but with each passing day, that chance gets less and less. If mankind could change the way it lives, if mankind were to put down its arms, then it could be averted. However, there is no sign that this will happen.

Some day someone will take matters into their own hands and will push the button, the button that will end civilization as you have come to recognize it.

Look to the sky. Tell those that you know who believe, to look up, that we are coming in greater numbers. We will do what we can. Tell those who believe, tell those who are righteous, that we are here, that we are watching over them, that we are praying for their safety.

There will be many signs to look for. The signs will differ depending upon what part of the earth you live on. When the earthquakes and volcanic eruptions start en masse, your sun and your moon will look different than they do now. There will be strange atmospheric conditions — a pink haze in the sky. This pink haze will cover everything so that when you see the moon, and when you see the sun, they will no longer appear the same to you. Also, the course of mighty rivers will be altered. One in South America will make headlines within the next few months. There will be a considerable number of earthquakes, some of which will even occur in your eastern United States. Though they have occurred before, this is the first time that such tremors of a very strong magnitude will be recorded.

IS NEW YORK GOING TO BE DESTROYED?

New York has already destroyed itself. As for a total physical destruction, this may occur, but there is a strong possibility that it will not, for it would take a very strong physical reaction to sink or tilt the island of Manhattan. This may occur before the end as we know it, but by that time, most of the people will already be evacuated who will be taken off the planet.

ARE THERE AREAS ON OUR PLANET WHICH WILL BE SAFE TO LIVE IN FOR AT LEAST A LITTLE WHILE?

There will be areas which you can go to that will be safe. Arizona is one such place that is frequently mentioned, and it is a good place. Also Wyoming, and Oklahoma, and perhaps the Dakotas.

You will know that the time has arrived to leave where you are when there is an increased number of UFOs seen in the sky. During the period just before the End Times, UFOs will be coming down here from many sources to watch these things, and at some point to lift off those people whose deeds are such that it makes it essential that they be taken along. These are the ones that we would have repopulate the earth at some future date. Also to be taken, are those that have particular skills or abilities and have no criminal record.

HOW MANY PEOPLE WILL BE TAKEN FROM THE EARTH?

Each group coming down here will be taking people off. Our own ships will be responsible for upwards of 20,000. We would estimate that altogether perhaps 140,000 to 170,000 people will be lifted up and taken off the planet.

THIS IS NOT VERY MANY CONSIDERING THE POPULATION OF THE WORLD

It is certainly true that this is not a great figure, but if the people on earth lived more according to the universal laws, the great catastrophes and holocaust would not take place. So why should we remove them, only to have the same thing start all over again? Also, the question arises if we were to take more than this, what would we do with these people? We would be responsible for their safety, for housing them, feeding them, and taking care of their various needs while they are away from the planet. It would be anywhere from five years to several decades before the earth is safe to be repopulated again. After the great war, if one should occur, we will send ships down that will clear the air of any radioactivity. The volcanic eruptions will probably simmer down in awhile. The earthquakes will also become less frequent because there will be a shifting, probably of the entire earth's axis. So the whole land mass will be reshaped entirely. There will be very few areas that will be able to stand the force of the holocaust. These few safe areas that we mentioned will only be safe in the beginning, as when the earth tilts on its axis, if that is what is to happen, whole land masses will be completely altered. But, it is from these areas that a good many of the people that will be picked up will be lifted off the earth.

WHERE WILL THESE PEOPLE BE TAKEN TO?

There will be several large cities in space, some of which your scientists have already observed. These ships which can house many,

many thousands of people will be put in orbit around the sun as if they were planets themselves. Then at the time the earth has been made stable again, the people will be brought back. These planets orbiting around the sun will be big enough so that people can go on living quite comfortably. Food will be grown there. There will be recreation and entertainment areas. There will be schools. There will be hospitals. Life will go on.

If you watch the news you can see that the earth is like a festering wound, a wound that keeps getting larger and larger. There is more hatred among mankind then ever before. The bomb is about ready to explode. But do not fear, be happy, be content, be glad that you are living in such an important era. And remember, watch the skies for we are here and we are watching over you. We send our love, we send our well wishes, we send our strength and our power to you and those who are deserving.

IF OUR LEADERS WERE TO ACKNOWLEDGE YOUR EXISTENCE COULD YOU IN ANY WAY BE ABLE TO ASSIST US?

Your planet would jump many years ahead in technology if your scientists and world leaders would simply acknowledge our presence. We have many things we would like to share with you that we could teach you, that you could learn from.

At this very moment, your energy, the energy that you have within the bowels of the earth, is depreciating. Very, very soon there will not be enough power for your cities to provide you with the energy you need for heat, for refrigeration.

The economics are very, very bad, not only in your own country, but in other countries as well. There are many unstable conditions which we could help improve.

And while these are troubled times, these are also good times for those who will open their minds, for those who would cast their eyes skyward, for those who look for our gleaming craft. For we come with knowledge, with love and peace in our hearts. It is very important that your world unite, for separated as it is now, it will eventually destroy itself. Unity is important.

One of the reasons that we are making select contacts at this time is to tell you that your planet cannot stand another world war. In a world war there would be no winner, every side would be the loser.

YOU MEAN NO ONE WOULD SURVIVE THE END TIMES HERE ON EARTH?

More than likely there will always be people on the earth. These catastrophies will take the lives of millions, but there will always be places for people to hide. In fact, there are now people who are living underground, people who are actually living inside your own planet, who once lived on the surface many eons ago. But they too nearly destroyed themselves. Some of them built rocketships to go into outer space, while others built cities underground.

UFOs are very important. We ask that you get the word out. We ask that you tell as many people as possible about the existence of flying saucers, for they are very important for your state of development. Readers should note that a portion of the above channeled communications have been excerpted from the text *The New World Order: Channeled Prophecies From Outer Space* issued by Inner Light Publications in a limited edition and hopefully it will be expanded into a full lenth book shortly.

RAISE THE COMING OF EARTH INTO THE FOURTH DIMENSION

As Phillel of Mark Age sees things there has to be a definite reason behind all that has and is about to transpire on Earth. To his way of thinking the New Agers are the ones to help bring about the landing of light into Earth's consciousness, for this the disciple of the *Mark Age* group sees as necessary before humanity can progress along the karmic wheel of spirituality — a path which the Federation of Planets is determined to guide us along in the years just up ahead.

Since these revelations are so important in the scheme of things it seems essential that we let Mark Age give us as much in the way of detail as possible. Thus the necessity to allow them to give a full accounting of what is to transpire in order to take the inhabitants of this planet of ours upward into the fourth dimension.

Thus let us proceed with this report from our friends at Mark Age:

* * *

CHAPTER SEVEN

A Blending Of Cosmic Souls

I n this chapter I hope to set forth some clues as to who the "Chosen Ones" among us actually are. We have been told over and over again that purity of thought is essential, as is honesty of heart. But if only a little over a hundred thousand individuals are to be "lifted up" on what basis will they be selected by the Space Brothers who are said to be watching over us? Let's see if we can't make some sense out of this.

Whenever I've asked the question, "Is there any particular reason why you feel you have been chosen for repeated contacts with alien beings?" I usually am given a similar response. Most UFO contactees can talk for hours about the philosophy of the outer space intelligence they communicate with, but they appear unusually naive as to why they should be the ones to carry forth this message to the public. Can it be, I've often wondered, that the UFOnauts simply pick people at random to establish prolonged contact with? Is being in the right place at the right time, all there is to this selection? I've always found this idea hard to believe.

"They told me they were coming back to contact their own," Barbara Hudson looked me directly in the eye and simply shrugged her shoulders. The attractive black woman had answered my question to the best of her ability, it was just that she didn't really know what the space people that she's been in touch with since she was a young girl, were talking about. "How can I be one of them?" she asks in total candor. "After all, I was born right here in the United States."

On many occasions contactees have told me pretty much the same thing not realizing what it is they are actually professing. Yet, when we take their statement and combine it with other fascinating data, the space people's coming back to contact their own starts to make amazing sense.

STAR PEOPLE

About eight years ago, as he traveled around the country while lecturing, well-known parapsychologist Brad Steiger, noticed that many men and women he met, actually claimed either to have strange memories of having come to this planet from "somewhere else," or to have experienced an interaction with paranormal entities since their earliest childhood. Steiger came to call these individuals "Star People" and noticed that they had many similar physical attributes and physiological anomalies which obviously placed them apart from the rest of society.

The pattern profile of the "Star People" contains the following elements:

UNUSUAL BLOOD TYPE.
LOWER BODY TEMPERATURE.
WAS AN UNEXPECTED CHILD.
EXTRA VERTEBRAE AND LOWER BACK PROBLEMS.
THRIVE ON LITTLE SLEEP.
APPEAR HYPERSENSITIVE TO ELECTRICITY, ELECTROMAGNETIC FORCE FIELDS.
UNUSUALLY SHARP HEARING AND EYES VERY SENSITIVE TO LIGHT.
FELT THEIR MOTHER AND FATHER WERE NOT THEIR REAL PARENTS.
COMPLAIN OF FEELING GREAT URGENCY,

BRAD & SHERRY STEIGER

A SHORT TIME TO COM-PLETE GOALS. LOW BLOOD PRES-SURE. CHRONIC SINUS-ITIS. FEEL THAT THEIR TRUE AN-CESTORS CAME FROM AN-OTHER WORLD, ANOTHER DIMEN-SION, AND THEY YEARN FOR THEIR TRUE PLACE OF ORIGIN.

Brad Steiger has authored 125 books, both hardcover and paper-back, covering such topics as UFOs, prophecy, astral projection, life after death, and ESP. He has also written scores of maga-zine articles, and at one time had a daily newspaper column syn-dicated here and abroad. A warm and friendly person, Brad has received his share of rewards for his outstanding contributions to a still-developing field. In October, 1974, he was awarded the coveted "Genie" as Best Metaphysical Writer of the Year. He is also one of the top speakers at conventions, seminars and on college campuses. Brad's first novel titled, "The Hypnotist" (a spellbinding story of reincarnation and evil) has been publish-ed by Dell.

HAD UNSEEN COMPANIONS AS A CHILD. NATURAL ABILITIES WITH ART, MUSIC, HEAL-ING, OR ACTING.

EXPERIENCE A BUZZING OR A CLICKING NOISE IN THEIR EARS PRIOR TO, OR DURING, SOME PSYCHIC EVENTS.

HAD AN UNUSUAL EXPERIENCE AROUND THE AGE OF FIVE WHICH OFTEN TOOK THE FORM OF A WHITE LIGHT AND/OR A VISITATION BY HUMAN-TYPE BEINGS WHO GAVE INFORMATION AND COMFORT.

HAVE SINCE MAINTAINED A CONTINUING SERIES OF EPISODES WITH "ANGELS," "ELVES," "MASTERS," OR OPENLY DECLARED UFO INTELLIGENCES.

THEIR ARTWORK OR DREAMS OFTEN INVOLVE A MULTI-MOON ENVIRONMENT.

CHILDREN AND ANIMALS ARE ATTRACTED TO THEM.

THEY DO THEIR BEST WORK AT NIGHT.

As Steiger correctly points out, despite a seemingly bizarre belief that they are not from here, these "Star People" all appear normal and rational otherwise. Most of the Star People Brad met were intelligent and highly articulate and sensed that they had a particular purpose or "mission" in life, though they might not have sorted out in their own mind what made them so "special."

Based upon his research, Steiger draws the conclusion that there was once a mixing of the genes between Earth men and women and beings from other worlds. He believes that this is what so many of the world's religions are referring to when they speak of the "Sons of God" or the "Star People" seeing that the "Daughters of Men were fair," went ahead and mated with them. Brad contends that the "Giants in the Earth" which resulted from these early unions were the ancestors of the Star People of today. And while such a "Cosmic Union" probably did take place eons ago, I believe that many of those who feel like they are "Strangers in a Strange Land" actually are *not* totally from this planet, but are "Blends," composed of both an earthly soul and the spirit of an alien entity.

Once you have a full understanding of this comment, Barbara

Hudson's statement which she attributes to her space contacts, "We are coming back to contact our own," starts to make remarkable sense. Furthermore, we begin to see just who it is among us who will be lifted off this planet during the closing out of this old, dying, period of materialism on earth.

A MODERN-DAY FEMALE MOSES

Back before that warm August night in 1974, Lydia Stalnaker was a very successful businesswoman who ran a modeling agency and spent most of her free time raising two daughters, Penny and Patty.

As Lydia crossed a rather remote section of highway between Jacksonville and Callahan, Florida, her life was destined to change drastically. Suddenly, from out of nowhere, a bright, flashing white light came into view just above the tree tops. "Upon driving nearer to the strange flashing light, I began to shake as if chilled and began to feel a tingle in my left arm. I began breathing hard as if something were closing in on me. It was a suffocating feeling as if something were taking control of me. Suddenly, my mind went blank and for how long I remained apparently unconscious, I do not know, but it seemed only a short period of time before I was conscious again. When I awoke, I noticed that I was driving along a totally different road than I had been on before sighting the strange object above the trees."

Three hours of Lydia's life disappeared that evening and were not remembered until May 1975 when Lydia underwent retrogressive hypnosis. Since that night in August, Lydia says she suffered from intense headaches and would cry and feel panic-stricken for no reason at all. "I thought I had gone crazy and could not understand what was happening to me."

Under hypnosis it came out that during the missing hours, Lydia had been taken aboard a space craft and placed on a table-like machine opposite another woman. "As I was being strapped into this table-like machine by unknown persons, I was told that they were going to try to place this other woman inside my body and that I would be like them and she would be like me. I was told that this process would not hurt badly. My head was then placed inside something and the table began to revolve. It turned faster and faster until I eventually passed out. When I awoke, I felt something warm coming through the top of my head and traveling through my entire body. The machine was stopped and the aliens seemed to be very happy about something. I heard them say that it had worked and they helped me off the table. One of the aliens placed a robe around my shoulders and said I was now *one of them*. He walked me to the door of the ship and said they would be in contact with me again."

Since the night this all happened, Lydia has developed telepathic powers to the point where she can read other people's thoughts. Beyond this heightened extrasensory perception, Lydia has also gone into the area of psychic healing with many testimonials, swearing that her abilities to cure various ailments are authentic.

Placed under hypnosis on subsequent occasions by Professor James Harder of UCLA, Lydia revealed that the alien woman who had been opposite her on the table-like machine was now occupying her body. Eventually, this alien personality was able to speak through Lydia's vocal cords and identified herself as Antron. Trying his best to mend what he must have thought was a split personality, Dr. Harder told the entity that it is impossible for more than one spirit to occupy the same body. To this Lydia — or Antron should we say — remarked: "We are as one. We both live in the same house." The spacewoman went on to say that Lydia had approved of this merging of souls.

Little by little Lydia's alien companion began to reveal bits and pieces pertaining to her own background. "My place is not of this solar system," Antron reflects, "but of another solar system called a star galaxy. All people of different origins know God. They have been taught that God is, as you would say, a missionary sent here. My planet is green from the outside, where earth is blue. We have better atmospheric layer conditions. We do not get the radiation from outside as earth does. Therefore, we do not age as rapidly."

Antron's sharing of Lydia's human body was not done merely as a casual whim, but for a very specific reason. "The earth is getting ready for another cataclysmic event," Antron warns. "We want to take the good people with us to recolonize elsewhere."

Because of what Antron has said, Lydia Stalnaker has come to think of herself as sort of a modern-day female Moses. "I'm here to lead the righteous to a new world in space," she insists. "They continue to refer to the time of great geographical changes in the structure of the earth similar to the Biblical prophecies. They tell of the time soon to come, when earth changes will occur. If they have been studying earth changes for a number of centuries, as they claim perhaps we should listen to their advice."

WALK-INS

If you have any type of sensitivity at all, Lydia's story must send chills up and down your spine. I've heard Antron speak in person through her, and I can tell you this spacewoman is definitely not part of a split personality, but is a real entity unto itself.

Actually, the blending of a strange spirit with another human being is not that unusual when you review literature in the field of psychic phenomenon. Writer Ruth Montgomery calls these beings "Walk-Ins" and describes how they have on many occasions actually shared the same body with otherwise normal individuals.

What places these "Walk-Ins" apart from instances of possession by evil spirits or demons is the fact that complete cooperation must be offered by the original spirit that occupies the human form.

This "agreement" can apparently take place prior to birth, during so-called "death bed" experience when the individual is out of his body, or during periods when he is asleep or unconscious. Now how's this for coincidence? Remember Barbara Hudson who we referred to earlier? Well, it seems that at the age of five or six she was playing in her parents backyard, when for no apparent reason she keeled over and was pronounced dead by the family doctor. Barbara remained "dead" for a brief while, but remarkably she eventually sat up and had absolutely no recollection of what had happened. Perhaps, it was during this period of time that a "deal" was struck up and an alien spirit blended with hers. When the space people she is in touch with say the reason they are communicating with her is because, "They are coming back to contact their own," they are telling the absolute truth even if they don't bother to explain the meaning of their words.

Another visitor to our planet, an entity called Ishcomar explains this "blending" process more completely. "By mutual agreement between a planetary dweller and an inhabitant of our craft, the knowledge and memory of one of us may be blended with one of your inhabitants without the loss of the receiver's identity. The one from our group only adds to the knowledge of the planetary dweller and the abandoned body (of the alien) is disseminated. This blending cannot take place without the agreement of the individual and necessarily the planetary dweller must agree and desire this blending. We seek therefore not to take but to give."

It seems that living on our world at this time is an army of "helpers" who will be trying their best to assist us and guide us through this shaky and traumatic period. Some of them may not even know who they are yet, but they will SOON learn!

CURED OF AILMENTS

What a wonderful sight it will be to see gigantic space ships picking up people from all over the world. According to Robert Short of the Solar Space Foundation, many of those who are "lifted up" will be cured of sickness and ailments of mind and body. "This will be as a result of rebalance, and the grace given by the Creative Source of Ageless Life." According to many sources, when the earth *is* ready to be repopulated once again our world will exist in a higher vibrational level and only those who are attuned properly will be able to survive here.

Jane Allyson, the New York-based channel who will eventually relocate in Arizona, says that psychically she has received the message that, "As consciousness is raised on earth this consciousness raising appears to the space people as a light-form and this specific light-form will lead them to us when the time comes." Doesn't this sound as if Jane is making reference to the human aura that supposedly surrounds every living thing? Perhaps they will know which of us to select by reading our aura as this is a good indication of our emotional state of mind as well as our physical and spiritual being. Jane adds that the space people will be working with our spirit guides to help us when the time of evacuation finally arrives. Summing up what she has been told, Ms. Allyson remarks, "The only protection we will have will be our consciousness. There will be no mind control on their part, only total understanding. There is no chance of anything going wrong, and everyone will be working for the cause of survival. Only those with raised consciousness will understand and survive."

As I understand it, after the holocaust is over and those who have been taken away and want to come back, return to the earth, our world will be a Utopia, a sort of Heaven brought down out of the clouds. A Golden Age will develop and man will live in peace and will go on living in perfect health for centuries to come. Much of this is stated in the Bible, but in slightly different terms. Its all a matter of interpretation, and what your concept of the universe is. I don't believe there is anything unholy about these statements we have made, its just that we are viewing them through Twentieth Century eyes and with a deep mystical knowledge.

HARMONY AND PEACE

One thing we can state with absolute certainty — no one who is a negative person will be permitted on board the evacuation ships. Thelma B. Terrell has been told by one of her space contacts, Commander Hatonn of the Space Council, that their ships are "environments of harmony and peace. There is quietness, cooperation and dignity. There is courtesy and devotional awareness within each being. This is the only attitude capable of continuance in the vibrational atmosphere present within our craft. The frequencies are so high that they would destroy any vibration of a lesser nature. It is not a matter of saying, 'This one may come, or this one must stay,' it is of frequencies and vibrations. Those who have learned to live in love, and to apply an attitude of love to all situations have thus prepared themselves for these coming days of turmoil. . . It is at this meeting point of love, that we can mingle with you and accept you into our midst and our ships for rescue."

Another of Thelma's regular contacts is a highly evolved being from the planet Arcturus which is part of a distant constellation. During a recent early morning channeling session this being revealed that ships from his world would be among those outer space vehicles to take away the survivors. Apparently, just like on a sinking boat at sea, the children will be taken first. "I reveal to you in this release that we shall call for the children first. For the children are guiltless and the children are the victims of the madness of the adult world surrounding them. We shall make a place on our ships and our places of refuge for the children, first. These souls who have dared to enter your world at such a time as this, deserve our love and care first of all. For they do not know hatred until they are taught to hate. They do not know to kill until they are taught to kill. They do not know of mass destruction until they are taught to destroy. Each living soul has it's identifying ray, it's link with it's own personal record on our great computers. Your children are not lost when they are with us. They will be rescued first, and await your coming. Many thousands of your children are special souls who have come to progress, to unfold, and participate in the dawn of a New World."

When you think about it seriously, it would make a lot of sense to evacuate children. Depending on how serious the situation is back here on earth, older people might have to stay away too long and would be quite elderly when the time does come to return. Also, children would be ideal to populate the New Earth the space people speak of as they will be open to new ideas, and values, and will not be old enough to remember the hate that raged in the hearts, and minds of the adult population.

As you can see, Thelma Terrell's contacts have some very intriguing things to tell us, a lot more than we have space for in this present book.

By now you should have a pretty good inkling of those who are slated to be spirited away in the last days of the End Times we are making a study of. It is necessary that we try to lift our vibrations as high as possible and show good faith. It would seem that amongst us now are those whose minds and souls are a near perfect blend of earthling and alien. These individuals — the "Star People" — will soon be faced with the reality of who they are (if they don't already know) and will be entrusted with the mission of getting the rest of us set to go on board those great star ships that will be hovering in the sky.

CHAPTER EIGHT

The Cosmic Countdown Has Begun

There is sufficient reason to believe that we have passed the Eleventh Hour on the countdown, and that the hands of the cosmic clock are pushing Midnight. Throughout our research, we are told to look for certain "Signs," which will alert us to the fact that time is running short. As previously stated, not even the space people know the *exact* hour, since the future is subject to change. This seems to confirm Matthew 24.29-36 for those who are interested in tying this in with Bible reference: "But of the day and hour knoweth no man, no not even the angels (space being?) of heaven." I find it rather fascinating that much of what has been revealed to us via extraterrestrial sources seems to be quite similar to religious text, both Christian as well as other sects. There seems to be almost a universal understanding that something very traumatic is going to happen during the period in which we now find ourselves.

Remember Ashtar's prediction several chapters back to the effect that there would be a strange haze in the atmosphere which would turn the moon and sun a weird color, making it difficult to

A channel for the Ashtar Command, Tuella sees the arrival of UFOs in our atmosphere as part of a large spiritual plan for the Earth.

tell the difference between day and night? Well, there are several references in the Bible to just such an event. Take for example Isaiah 13.9-10: "For the stars of heaven and the constellations thereof shall not give their light; the sun shall be darkened . . . and the moon shall not cause her light to shine." Or take Amos 8.9: "And it shall come to pass in that day, sayeth the Lord, that I will cause the sun to go down at noon, and I will darken the earth in the clear day." Nor should we forget Joel 3.15 which says: "The sun and the moon shall be darkened, and the stars shall withdraw their shining."

To an extent, we might have already been given a sample of what could happen on a much larger, more intense scale. On several occasions in recent years pollution caused by waste being released into the atmosphere has cut visibility down to less than a foot in several large cities. The above photo was taken in the middle of the afternoon in Rockville, Maryland and serves as only a small indication of what is possible when man decides to go against Mother Nature. One day soon we could very easily have the three days of darkness spoken of so often in prophecy and we will know with a strong conviction in our heart that the End Times are upon us.

MYSTERY MESSAGES

Another sure-fire sign that we are approaching the close of an age, and that extraterrestrial intervention (to whatever degree is allowed) is at hand, is said to be the taking over of our broadcasting facilities by the UFOnauts. According to the messages channeled for the past several decades, our space friends will interfere with our normal radio and television reception, and will issue a communication directly to the people of earth. Supposedly, they will "cut in" over our regularly scheduled programs and will issue forth a proclamation that will be seen and heard in every country around the world. Thelma Terrell has recently received one such channeled message which deals with this precise subject: "Our technology is readied to super-impose our frequencies over your television and radio broadcasting systems if necessary, to reach the masses in the quickest possible manner. We can also extend our frequencies into your telephone lines for a brief message . . . We have systems similar to your public address systems, available from the smaller scout ships which operate with a volume and power unheard of in your technology. We have many ways of reaching quantities of persons simultaneously. We project into your thinking at this very date, that fear of us and our presence or our appearance, or lack of understanding of our motivation, will combine to produce such a negative field around your physical form that we would be unable to assist you." The channel then goes on to say, once again, that time is short. "We cannot promise you another decade. We cannot even promise you all of this one. Your destiny is in your hands." Pretty explicit words wouldn't you agree?

As an experiment to prove to us that such a massive take over of our communications systems can be accomplished, the UFOnauts have already beamed several important messages over our television stations.

The following is a complete transcript of the "Voice from Outer Space" as broadcast on TV, in the Hennington area of Southern England at 5:05 P.M. on Saturday, November 26, 1977.

"This is the voice of Glon, representative of the 'Asteron Galactic Command,' speaking to you. For many years you have seen us as lights in the sky. We speak to you now in peace and wisdom as we have done to your brothers and sisters all over this, your planet.

"We come to warn you of the destiny of your race in your world so that you may communicate to your fellow beings the course you must take to avoid disaster which threatens your world and the beings of other worlds around you.

"This is the order that you may share in the great awakening as the planet passes into the New Age of Aquarius. The New Age can be a time of great evolution for your race, but only if your rulers are made aware of the evil forces that can overshadow their judgement. Be still now, and listen, for your chance may not come again for many years.

"Your scientists, governments and generals have not heeded our warnings. They have continued to experiment with the evil forces of what you call nuclear energy. Atomic bombs can destroy the Earth and the beings of your sister worlds in a moment. The wastes from atomic power systems will poison your planet for many thousands of years to come. We who have followed the path of evolution for far longer than you, have long since realized this, that atomic energy is always directed against life. It has no peaceful application. Its use and research into its use must be ceased at once, or you will all risk destruction. All weapons of evil must be removed.

"The time of conflict is now passed and the races of which you are a part may proceed to the highest planes of evolution, if you show yourselves worthy to do this. You have but a short time to learn to live together in peace and good will. Small groups all over the planet are learning this and exist to pass on the light of a new dawning, the New Age to you all. You are free to accept or reject their teachings, but only those who learn to live in peace will pass to the higher realms of spiritual evolution.

"Hear then the voice of Glon — the voice of the 'Asteron Galactic Command' speaking to you. Be aware also that there are many false prophets and guides at present operating on your world. They will suck your energy from you, the energy you call money, and will put it to evil ends, giving you worthless gross in return. Your inner divine self will protect you from this. You must learn to be sensitive to the voice within that can tell you what is truth and what is confusion, chaos and untruth. Learn to listen to the voice of truth which is within you and you will lead yourself onto the path of evolution.

"This is our message to you, our dear friends. We have watched you growing for many years, just as you have watched our lights in the skies. You know now that we are here and that there are more beings on and around your Earth than your scientists care to admit. We are deeply concerned about you and your path towards the light and we will do all we can to help you. Have no fears, seek only to know yourself and live in harmony with the ways of your planet Earth.

"We are the 'Asteron Galactic Command'; thank you for your attention. We are now leaving the planes of your existence. May you be blessed with supreme love and truth of the cosmos."

Wouldn't you agree that this is a most inspiring communication? The authorities attempted to attack the validity of the message, stating that a vandal had taken over a deserted transmitter in a wooded area of the city and had somehow managed to broadcast the message, overriding the normal TV signal. What the spokesman for the television station neglected to mention is that there was actually more than one message, and they lasted for a considerable period of time, not the 15 or 20 seconds they tried to make everyone believe.

Lately, I have received a number of letters from subscribers to UFO REVIEW, a flying saucer publication which I have published for many years, who claim to be picking up strange "alien communications" on their ham radios. Many of these messages deal with end time prophecies and many of the things talked about in this book.

It's hard to believe that hoaxers got hold of some very expensive equipment and transmitted just for the "fun" of it. More likely, these messages fit right into the puzzle we are trying so desperately to solve.

"VALUABLES" TO BRING ALONG

Naturally, if the world blows up, turns to ashes, or flips on its axis, all the tea — or *money* — in China won't be of any use to survivors. Yet, if your house is burning down, or you are on a ship and it is sinking, you usually don't leave behind all your valuables. Its human nature to take that which is dearest to you, or that which you have worked the hardest for. If our cities collapse and we have to take to the road, as has been predicted, what should we make certain to take with us?

Chicago psychic Warren Freiberg has a few thoughtful suggestions on this matter. "Forget about taking money with you. Paper money and even coins won't be worth anything," he points out. "Food will be scarce and people won't want to part with what they have in exchange for worthless currency. Remember a dollar bill isn't worth anything in itself, its only valuable because the U.S. Government stands behind it. In all likelihood the government as we know it will be dissolved or at least totally ineffective to the point where nobody will be willing to listen to our former leaders as they will come to see the folly of their ways. If possible start saving things like silver and gold pieces, and also gems. Such items are always of value, but best of all they are relatively small and easy to carry on your person. My suggestion would be to turn your savings into diamonds or small gold coins. Eventually, the banks will shut down and all your life savings will go down the drain, so do something about it before its too late."

Robert Short's space contacts have informed him during several channeling sessions that the bartering system may be returned in the Last Days. "If you recognize that all have their methods, and thus if they return to their original teaching, which teaches abstinence from those paths which lead only to wrongdoing, and that which has replaced the people's ability to trade among themselves in humility and honesty, which is called a 'barter system.' They (the banking system and governments) have replaced this with that force which is MONETARY and thus have sold men's minds, bodies and souls into slavery upon your planet. If this ceased among the nations, then will peace come, not rapidly, but it will begin to replace the wrongdoing which had begun centuries before in your time when those of the human had placed value upon metals and gems, and other methods of exchange — in lieu of that which was the original verbal agreement and handshake between neighbors who were able to trade in true value among themselves..." This message was received on February 2, 1979, and in recent conversations, the head of the Solar Space Foundation has revealed that a return to the barter system may become a way of life before the end of our age.

When the time comes to be taken aboard a space ship for a quick trip out of this manmade hell, several of the space entities who have spoken through our channels agree that its alright to bring your personal necessities. "There are many personal items you might desire, which we could not provide, and if these few small things will make you content and happy while you wait, then they should be included. Your own ingenuity will be exercised here, keeping the contents few but vital," remarks Capt. Avalon of the Interplanetary Council.

So remember, keep a small overnight bag packed under your bed and ready to go. I can't say for certain, but they might not have your favorite brand of toothpaste in the outer reaches of the solar system.

SIGNS AND WONDERS

There is only one man I know of who is knowledgeable when it comes to UFOs and believes their mission is an honorable one, and is also a practicing evangelist who has placed his faith in God. Most religious leaders will tell you that flying saucers are the devil's messengers and that when they promise to save us they are only lying. Most ministers and clergymen have

Frank Stranges

not made a serious study of the UFO mystery, because they are dead set against it from the very beginning.

Frank Stranges is quite different in this regard. Not only is he a man of the cloth, but this evangelist claims to have actually met and conversed with a being from another planet. Several years back, Stranges was introduced to a spaceman who said his name was Val Thor, and that he had been living on earth for several years attempting to establish contact with the heads of government. Stranges claims that he spoke to Val Thor in the Pentagon, where the human-looking alien had been staying after proving his superiority and the fact that he came from an advanced civilization. In addition to his church work, Dr. Stranges is the only preacher I know to actually run a UFO group, the National Investigations Committee on Unidentified Flying Objects, which is located at 7970 Woodman Avenue, Van Nuys, California 91402.

Though much of Frank Stranges' teaching is based upon Biblical scripture, he is also familiar with the plan that the UFO intelligence has in store for us, and is thus able to incorporate his thinking on the matter of the End Times. According to Dr. Stranges a third world war is not that far off. He believes the next global conflict will involve Israel, the Arab states, the countries of Western Europe, the USSR, and the United States. This is how he sees the order of events transpiring in the Last Days:

1. MILLIONS WILL VANISH FROM THE FACE OF THE EARTH.
2. CHILDREN WILL BE REPORTED MISSING (remember the prediction that the Space Brothers will take our youngsters first), LOVED ONES GONE, GRAVES OPENED.
3. DISTRESS OF NATIONS, SUCH AS NEVER BEFORE TRANSPIRED ON THIS PLANET.
4. TRANSPORTATION WILL BE A MAJOR PROBLEM.
5. FROM THIS POINT ON, A SERIES OF PRESIDENTIAL ORDERS WILL BE ISSUED TO THE AUTHORITIES ON THIS PLANET, PLACING EVERY LIVING PERSON IN THE U.S. UNDER COM-

PLETE DICTATORSHIP!
6. ONCE THE "CHOSEN" HAVE BEEN REMOVED, THE PRESIDENT WILL:
   A. Take over all communication media.
   B. Take over all petroleum, gas, fuel, electric power, etc.
   C. Take over all food resources, farms, etc.
   D. Take over all modes of transportation, highways, airports.
   E. Mobilize all civilians into work forces under government supervision.
   F. Take over all health, welfare and education.
   G. Postmaster authorized to conduct nationwide registration of ALL persons.
   H. Take over all airplanes, aircraft, including private planes.
   I. Take over all housing, financing — to relocate people, build with public funds in certain designated areas.

While touring California several years ago I had the pleasure to be invited by Dr. Stranges to speak at his Saturday night lecture program in Van Nuys. After the evening's official schedule had been concluded Frank and I wandered down the hall to the seclusion of his private office for a more personal chit chat. Here we discussed some of his personal transformational views which incorporate the following earthly changes he sees as being on our door step. As we get nearer to the midnight hour — Frank paints a frightening apocalyptic vision that he believes will unfold all around us in the Earth, in the Heavens and in the stars. He sees his vision as being backed up by both orthodox Biblical teachings as well as being verified thorugh the channelings and thinking of many contemporary New Age teachers. Here is his breakdown on what events are likely to occur in nature.

THE SUN

Jesus said: *Immediately after the tribulation of those days shall the sun be darkened,* (Matt. 24:29).

The Apostle John was shown an apocalyptic vision of the world during the last days of the Great Tribulation, and he wrote that because of the sun . . . *men were scorched with great heat* . . . (Rev. 16:9).

The Prophet Isaiah wrote of this time, *the light of the sun shall be sevenfold, as the light of seven days.* (Isaiah 30:26).

For many years astronomers concluded that our sun could maintain its present heat-energy output for at least 8 million more years, because its hydrogen supply was only about half exhausted. However, more recently, some astronomers have reappraised this theory, and now believe that once a star (our sun is a medium size star) has expended half its hydrogen, it is in danger of experiencing a nova. Larger stars supernova (blow up) and the smaller stars, like our own, sun, nova — get brighter and hotter for a period of from 7 to 14 days, and then become darker. There are about 14 novas a year in the observable universe. Some astronomers now believe that the increased sun-spot activity is a sign that our own sun may be about to nova. The increased solar storm activity predicted could be the trigger that would set off the atomic collapse of the sun. A nova of our sun would most assuredly: (1) cause the sun to become unusually bright (as Isaiah prophesied) (2) become seven times hotter as John prophesied, and (3) then become dark as Joel and Jesus prophesied.

MOON

Isaiah prophesied:. . . *the light of the moon shall be as the light of the sun. . .,* (Isaiah 30:26).

Joel said of this time, *The sun shall be turned into darkness and the moon into blood. . .,* (Joel 2:31).

Jesus said,. . . *The sun shall be darkened, and the moon shall not give her light. . .,* (Matt 24:29).

Inasmuch as the moon has no light of its own, and reflects only that light which it receives from the sun, the prophetic word is in perfect harmony with science. It naturally follows that when the sun becomes 7 times brighter, as Isaiah prophesied, reflected light upon the earth will make the night as hot and bright as the average day. Then, when the sun becomes dark, as Jesus said it must, the moon will naturally give off no light. However, Joel indicates that at this time the moon will be turned into blood, or become red in appearance. The prophecy of Joel about the moon could well take place as the scientists believe there will be strange lighting effects in the heavens at our time.

EARTH

The environmental changes on earth preceding the return of Jesus Christ, will be varied and severe.

Storms: The Scriptures indicate that terrible storms and floods will occur at the beginning. We have always been of the opinion that the battle of Ezekiel 38 occurs at the first of the *Tribulation Period.* We read in verse 22 of great hailstones and an overflowing rain. It is also prophesied in Revelation 16:21, that upon men will fall. . .*a great hail out of heaven, every stone about the weight of a talent. . .* A talent is equal to about 10 pounds. A sudden shift in the winds with increased velocity conjointly with great disturbances in the upper atmosphere as predicted by scientists.

Drought: After the sudden shift in wind directions and temperature, resulting in violent storms, the wind will stabilize and a drought will prevail over the earth. Joel prophesied of the time of great distress, *The seed is rotten under their clods. . .How do the beasts groan! The herds of cattle are perplexed, because they have no pasture. . .The beasts of the field cry also unto thee: for the rivers of water are dried up. . .*(Joel 1:15-20).

We read in Revelation. . .that no rain will fall upon the earth for 1,260 days (about 3½ years), and could be a factor responsible for the world's changing weather pattern. It is significant, in the light of the Bible prophecy, that the scientists predict *great disrupting weather patterns around the globe.*

Time: Jesus said of the time factor during the *Great Tribulation,* . . .*And, except those days should be shortened, there should no flesh be saved. . .* The duration of the Tribulation Period is already established by God. It will be 7 years — no more and no less. The last half of the Tribulation Period also called the *Time of Jacob's Trouble,* will be 3½ years (42 months — Rev. 13:5). Calendar-wise, the Great Tribulation cannot be shortened. Therefore, it seems obvious that Jesus was referring to the shortening of the hours of the days (literally, the days themselves will be shortened by several hours.) The evident truth of Jesus' prophecy is verified in Rev. 8:12, . . .*and the day shone not for a third part of it, and the night likewise.*

Earth's Orbit: The Scriptures indicate that before the flood, rain did not fall upon the ground. The earth was watered by a mist. A layer of water vapor in the upper atmosphere served as an air-conditioner, and there was an even temperature from pole to pole. Then this vapor was removed at the flood, the earth tilted on its axis 23 degrees, and a great amount of this water was frozen at the ice caps. The resulting change in environment decreased the life span of man from several hundred years to three score and ten. We read in the 34th chapter of Isaiah, *that at the time. . . the Lord of hosts shall reign in mount Zion and Jerusalem, and before his ancients gloriously* (verse 23), that *The earth shall reel to and fro like a drunkard* (verse 20). There is an excellent probability the earth will be righted on its axis and preflood conditions restored. During the Millennium, we are informed by the Scriptures that all deterrents to a fruitful earth will be removed, and people shall live to be several hundred years old (Isaiah 65:19-25).

Famine: Jesus prophesied of the last days. . .*and there shall be famines. . .* (Matt 24:7). World health and food experts have predicted that from 1975 to 1985, one billion people could starve to death. Already, 28 nations around the equatorial belt have experienced drought and famine for the past 3 years. This assuredly, will have an effect on agriculture, and make feeding the exploding population of the earth more difficult. If drastic weather changes take place as predicted, then the expected one billion victims of famine within the next ten years may be a conservative estimate.

Earthquakes: Jesus said also of signs related to His Second Coming *and there shall be. . . earthquakes in diverse places.* Jesus meant that at the time of the end of this age, earthquakes would occur in increasing numbers in many places. It is remarkable that scientists have warned, there will be many earthquakes, large and small. These are almost the exact words that Jesus chose to describe of one of the judgments that would be visited upon the earth at the time of His return. As much is said about earthquakes in the end of the age as any other heavenly or earthly phenomena during the Great Tribulation. Revelation 6:12. . .*There was a great earthquake; and the sun became black. . . and the moon became as blood.* (Revelation 11:13), *And the same hour there was a great earthquake, and the tenth part of the city (Jerusalem) fell, and in the earthquake were slain of men seven thousand. . .* (Revelation 16:18.20). . . *and there was a great earthquake such as was not since men were upon the earth so mighty an earthquake, and so great. . . and every island fled away, and the mountains were not found.*

SIGNS IN THE EARTH

Scientists say that there will be drastic weather changes; fierce changing winds: rapidly accelerating solar activity connected with an outward gravitational pull that may cause the earth to become exceedingly hot for several days; the ice caps may melt and earthquakes occur all over the earth. If the predictions of the scientists measure up to even 26 percent of expectations, then soon there may be a time of desolation and tribulation. Jesus said of His coming again, as recorded in Luke 21:25—28, that there would be *fearsome signs in the heavens and upon the earth, distress of nations.*

Since 1945 the world has witnessed on several occasions the rising of pillars of smoke and fire into the atmosphere from the explosion of nuclear devices. Joel said this would be one of the signs of the last days.

As we have already brought out, earthquakes will be only a part of the drastic environmental changes on earth that scientists believe will take place. However, earthquakes are perhaps the most important from a Biblical standpoint, because earthquakes have always signified dispensation changes in God's dealings with mankind. There must have been great earthquakes at the flood, because we read in Genesis 7:11 . . . *that the fountains of the great deep were broken up.* There must have been another great earthquake at the time that God divided the nations at the time of the Tower of Babel. God divided the nations by race, languages, and cultures; and He divided them by mountains, rivers, seas, deserts and oceans. Science has now verified that the continents were all one huge land mass, but something happened and they broke up and floated apart. For example, the east coast of South America fits like a puzzle piece against the west coast of Africa. And if you will consult an earthquake map of the fault lines around the world, they generally follow the coasts of the continents, indicating that a great earthquake most likely caused the continents and islands to separate.

DAYS OF DARKNESS

This channeled message has been circulated among various groups and individuals and purports to be directly from The Christ. It was received through Anna, the prophetess who considers herself a messenger of God. We fully realize it is of a controversial nature and present it because so many have expressed interest in material regarding specifically "THE DAYS OF DARKNESS" so many have predicted. Interestingly, it is quite similar to other such channeled messages being received worldwide.

* * *

This is thy Lord, Jesus Christ. I have spoken of three phases of Cleansing. The first is the three days of Darkness; the second is the Seven-Year Famine; and the third is the Battle of Armageddon, at which time the Children of God will not be on earth, but will have been evacuated.

There have been cleansings in which there were three days of darkness in the time of Noah; and in the time of the flight of the Children of Israel out of Egypt; and in the time of Enoch; and in the time of Abraham. When Abraham was, the earth had existed twenty-six hundred years, but there was no written history. The history of the earth is written in God's Book of Life, where those who can go to the Akashic Records can read it. Atlantis was at the time of Enoch. Lemuria was at the time of the flight of the Children of Israel out of Egypt.

When ye see this writing, the time will be short before the beginning of the first cleansing. When the three days of darkness begin, it is well to think only thoughts of love and kindness to all that cross your mind. This will alleviate the pressure of unforgiven feelings. Those who are not able to cope with the hearing of these events are not yet right in their love relationship with God. When a person knows God is in charge of all things at all times, they can cope with anything God plans for them or the earth. They may be somewhat frightened, but will receive comfort and guidance by looking to God.

When the first Cleansing begins, it will be on a clear day in the middle of the day. The sun will fade away and darkness will begin to come over the land. There will be several hours before total darkness will be on all sides. There will be time for all enlightened to bring home their family; put water and feed outside for their animals and birds; and obtain supplies of food which does not need to be prepared and clean drinking water where it can be reached in the dark. Have warm clothing and bedding to remain wrapped in for the duration of the darkness, which will last three days. By the third night stars will be seen in the heavens. The fourth day the sun will shine again. During these three days of utter darkness, it is necessary that those in the houses do not look outside. It is necessary that they cover their windows with heavy covers which keep out the cold and keep the warmth inside.

The light that can be used for a short period of time has to be a battery-operated light. No fires or open flame light is to be used in the first three days. This will use up oxygen, which is already low in the atmosphere of the earth. Those who have respiratory problems will have a difficult time surviving. It is well if the door not be opened to anyone or for any reason. After the first three days, candles may still not be used for two more days; then ye can use any light or heat ye wish. Electricity should be re-established in a matter of time after the sun shines again. You can use whatever light or heat ye wish after the first three days, but are required to stay inside your home another eleven days without opening the doors or looking out the windows. This is to know only that which is in thy house. The memory of the outside would not be easily removed.

The commodes should flush the entire time. The freezers will be off during the time the electricity is off. Food could be spoiled; test before eating. Not all those who are outside of God's care will leave the body. Some will live through it through sheer perseverance on their part — *the will to live*. This terrible thing must happen because the people have hardened their hearts. At the close of each age a cleansing is necessary. We are in the transitional period between the Piscean Age and the incoming Aquarian Age.

Those who will keep their animals inside to protect them will suffer the consequence of disobedience. God is not mocked. There is reason for what He asks of the people of the earth who have gone far astray from His laws. The animals are cared for by my beings, who are on earth for this reason. None will die. This cleansing is not for the animals or for little children. The little children who are left on earth without their parents are in God's care. The Angels will care for and comfort the little ones. There will very quickly be found loving homes for them to be raised in. The parents with little ones need not worry how they will be cared for. God's plan is complete.

After the three days of darkness are past, stay inside another eleven days. This is to re-establish the atmosphere on the earth and to give the Space Brothers sufficient time to take care of the debris the destruction has caused, and to remove the bodies of those who are no longer living. When the people come out of their houses on the fourteenth day, they will see no sign of the terrible things that happened. These will have been through a cleansing in their terrible experience, and will now accept God into their lives.

When the sun shines on the fourth day, those who are yet alive need to thank God. It is not better to be dead than alive when God is carrying out a cleansing plan on the earth. When they are yet alive, they have yet an opportunity to establish a closer walk with God which will assure them a safer place in God's kingdom. By safer, I mean an area where God's laws are yet obeyed. After the three days of darkness and before the Battle of Armageddon, is a time when the people will wish to learn how to obey that which God has said they can do as the Lord Jesus Christ is able to do. When the aftermath of this terrible destruction is past, the world will then be in a famine for seven years. During these seven years the church and the school will be established with the help of Angelic guidance. In the time given for this activity, these lessons will be learned sufficiently that those who come back to earth will bring back the knowledge and the talents which they took with them. After that will follow the Battle of Armageddon. Those who are in God's care are not on earth during this time. They will have been taken up with me into a beautiful and peaceful area where they will stay until the aftermath of the last battle on earth is cleared away. Then chosen ones will be returned to earth the same way they were taken. This will be done by our Space Brothers and their spaceships. One phase will go directly into the next. The Children of God will not be brought back until the debris of all the cleansing is cleared away and the earth is fresh and clean. The Children of God will have been in a state of heaven, and will have forgotten happenings on the earth. They will be taken with their bodies and brought back with their bodies. Nothing at all will be left on earth. Some things of this civilization will be found hundreds of years from now, or even thousands, and will be called "Artifacts of the Lost Civilization of Earth."

When the Children of God are returned again to earth, they will be beamed back asleep and will awaken on earth in an area close to where they were when they were taken up. They will not remember it but many will feel comfortable with their atmosphere, as if they had been there before. They will arrive in comfortable weather and will have nothing with them except some tools which the Space Brothers will leave with each adult. With these tools they will slowly begin to carve out a pattern for life. They will begin to plant seeds which will be left for them. They will carve dishes out of wood. They will build fires to keep warm and to cook food. They will find vegetables and fruit growing and seeds and nuts, and things which grew in the area when they were taken away. It will be much like the Garden of Eden.

The Children will have Angels and Space Brothers with them on earth to help them build homes; establish the various systems such as government, financial, educational, and the system in which people are made well when something affects them adversely. This will not be a medical system in which doctors use chemical and other harmful procedures for which they can charge an exorbitant price from the already impoverished patient or the patient's family. This healing system is called "The Well-Making by Mental Power." Each person will learn how to apply his own mental powers to all phases of his life. When a person is too ill to accomplish this, there will be practitioners who will help the patient heal himself by directing the patient's thoughts.

My thoughts will be picked up by all when I am giving them guidance or comfort. This they will have learned in the interim between the time they were taken and the time they are brought back.

When the Children of God come back they are no longer called by the name they had when they were taken. They will have forgotten. In time they will think of something to call each other. They cannot read or write now. The schools must teach this very soon. The Angels will teach the teachers and build places to learn in.

There will be animals of other kinds; some were on earth before. There will be no vicious animals. All animals will love each other as people do.

The only supplies people will have will be those they can find around them. They will soon learn to make clothes to cover them up and keep them warm on cold nights. They will come back with the clothes they had on when they were taken. The weather will not be cold for some time — that is, until the people have learned to make clothes and bedding for themselves to protect them against the elements. Their God would not bring bad things upon them without giving them a way to protect themselves.

The Angels will have similar flesh bodies as they did at the time the Sons of God were upon the earth and found the daughters of man very fair, and loved them and had children with them. There will be children born of these attractions, who will be normal children. The fathers will disappear, one after another, when their work is done. The mothers of the children will know their husband was a Son of God and would be leaving again. They will raise the children with love and loving memories of their fathers. The children will be the same in all ways as are children on earth.

To get to this beautiful Garden of Eden with God and the Angels, one must now give his or her heart to God to be forgiven and guided by God into a life of service to God.

Those returning will be much wiser and purer in mind and body. They are then given a piece of ground and tools to make their living and to learn to survive with the help of the Angels which God is sending with them to guide, guard, protect, comfort, and supply their needs. The tools and other equipment are not of the earth kind. This is the age when God is ruling in the hearts and lives of those on earth. They will live closely with their Angels. The Angels will be protectors and companions to them. The people will have learned to communicate with God and with the Angels assigned to them by their Lord, Jesus Christ. The Angels are an ever-present help in all things.

Those who return to earth will have no recall of their families or homes. The healing work will have been done in them while they are where they awaited return to earth. People of all ages will return.

Those who have family with them will stay with their kinfolk though they will not know they are kin. This will keep family love and ties between them. Those who are without family will be grouped in a way that they can soon become family. Their Angels will be a great help in this area. The Angels will express much love to them and create a feeling of togetherness by a bond.

Space Brothers are highly evolved Beings of great light who operate space vehicles to do the work which God requires in all areas of the Universe. They are involved with this very important work on earth. They live in their vehicles when they are not based doing clean-up work. They wear uniforms which resemble those of an army. The uniforms are not clothing; they are of a substance which is formed over the wearers. The Space Brothers do not have names except when they are assigned to a person or a group who can communicate with them. The name is relinquished when their work with that person or group is finished. The name is given to them by God and usually denotes a status. The spaceships also have names at that time.

The time is now when those who have the light of understanding need to heed this message and prepare the best they can. Where there is not enough money because of the economy to buy that which they need, and their heart is with God, they can count on their Angels providing that which they need. They will find they need less than they think. Their Angels have many ways to bring necessary things to them. In the wilderness the Children of Israel were given quail when the Children were tired of spiritual food and were complaining loudly to God. Spiritual food is fruits and vegetables, nuts, seeds, honey, and grains. There was plenty of that for them. Before they left Egypt they were eating meat, and they thought they needed meat to have strength to travel. They did not need meat, but God gave it to them because they *thought* they needed it.

Meat-eating is against God's laws for man. In the coming age, God will re-establish this battered law. There will be no eating of the flesh of any of His animal kingdom; neither will their skins be used for clothing for man. This was never the intent of God's animal kingdom. God has permitted it to be until this time because men learned to depend on animal flesh when Noah and his family came off the ark and found no food. Then God said, "Take an animal and kill it and stay alive." Since that time, man has enjoyed eating the flesh of God's animals, but the time is now when God will reclaim His animals as He is reclaiming His souls. God is staging a final campaign to give the souls who have free will, the choice to come. If the animals had a choice, they would choose not to be slaughtered and eaten by man. They also have intelligence and feelings, and emotions, as does man.

With this message which is given by me, thy Lord, Jesus Christ, *THE PEOPLE HAVE BEEN WARNED.* Those who have given their hearts and lives to God are in God's care and are surrounded by His Angels. Only those who are yet outside of God's care have a great worry.

THE HOPI PROPHECIES

As we have repeatedly tried to communicate throughout this book, it is not one particular sect, cult or religious denomination, that is responsible for these forecasts of doom. Just about every culture on earth seems to realize that we are treading on very dangerous water, and that the future looks quite bleak.

For example, the great American Indian tribe, the Hopi feel strongly about this subject. Several years ago the Hopi Indian prophets attempted to get inside the United Nations in New York, where they could present their findings regarding the End Times (based upon a sacred stone tablet which the tribe has had for many generations) to the General Assembly, and ask that the White Man's ways be  mended before it is too late. Said Chief Dan Katchongva, "Many people, living at this time, will live to see the White Brother return to the earth, and when they do they will live to consider what they could have heard if they had permitted the original inhabitants of these, the Americas, to give a message to that great body of people." Chief Katchongva was not allowed to deliver his End Times message to the U.N. delegates, and for this he voiced his sad concern. The following Hopi prophecies are given as signs by this American Indian tribe, that we should all be aware of:

1. A SERIES OF EARTHQUAKES WILL BE FELT THROUGHOUT THIS LAND, AND WILL COME AS WARNINGS TO THE PEOPLE TO REPENT, IF THEY DO NOT HEED THESE WARNINGS AND REPENT BEFORE IT IS TOO LATE, A BAD EARTHQUAKE WILL STRIKE, DEVASTATING MANY CITIES AND RESULT IN THE DEATH OF LARGE MASSES OF PEOPLE.

2. FLOODS WILL BE SEEN IN PLACES WHERE THEY HAVE NEVER BEEN SEEN BEFORE.

3. THERE WILL BE A GREAT CLIMATICAL CHANGE WORLDWIDE; HOT/COLD, DRY/WET, IN EACH CASE IT WILL BE THE WORST IN RECORDED HISTORY.

4. THERE WILL BE FAMINE, PESTILENCE, DISEASE, AND PLAGUE THROUGHOUT THE LAND.

5. THE HOPI WERE WARNED NEVER TO DEPEND UPON

GREAT INVENTION THAT WOULD BE BROUGHT TO THEM BY THE WHITE RACE, THEY WERE TOLD THAT A LIGHTING SYSTEM WOULD BE ESTABLISHED THORUGHOUT THE LAND, AND ALL ONE HAD TO DO WAS TOUCH THE WALL TO LIGHT THE ROOM, HOWEVER, ONE DAY, WE WERE TOLD, THIS SYSTEM WOULD BE CUT OFF AT ONCE, AND THE PEOPLE WOULD BE LEFT IN PANIC. WE WERE ALSO WARNED AGAINST RUNNING WATER THAT WOULD COME INTO OUR HOMES. THIS WATER WILL BE POLLUTED AND ANYONE DEPENDING ON IT WILL DIE OR GET TERRIBLY SICK.

6. THERE WILL BE TERRIBLE FIGHTING ALL OVER THE LAND, CITY AGAINST CITY, VILLAGE AGAINST VILLAGE, AND FAMILY AGAINST FAMILY, THE HOPI WERE WARNED TO STAY ON THEIR RESERVATION.

7. THE MOON WILL TURN TO BLOOD, AND THE SUN WILL HIDE ITS FACE WITH SHAME.

8. THE SEASONS WILL CHANGE, AND ICE WILL FLOW FROM THE NORTH COUNTRIES.

The Hopi's believe that a messiah, a true white brother wearing a red cap and red cloak, will return to the earth and will try to straighten out our affairs for us. Apparently, the Hopi's are quite familiar with UFOs, and have seen them many times hovering over their hunting grounds, and later near their reservations. Their legends taken into consideration the fact that we are not the only intelligent beings to reside in God's universe.

Many great American Indian leaders have developed as spiritual leaders in the last few years, and there are an even increasing number of New Agers who are starting to accept the idea that the American Indian may at least be in part responsible for the safety of many during the coming turbulance. Sun Bear and Rolling Thunder have spoken widely on this theme and their writings have become very popular.

Harley Swiftdeer has lectured widely on the theme of the Red Man in prophecy and the increasing role of the medicine man — or shaman. A true visionary, Swiftdeer has, along with other Indian seers, put together a picture of what is to occur between now and the year 2000.

"These prophecies," says Harley Swiftdeer, "are a dream that is potential reality. It is not an ultimatum. But it is ours to behold and to create if we only dare to dream it together."

THE VISION

"The next few years are critical. And the reason for this is that for three years seeds of light have been planted and we are starting to grow and the teachings are starting to come out and all those ones inside each of the Eight Great Powers who have taught partial truths, who have taught deliberate lies in myth, who have used the power of wheels to gain control of people to gain followers, to gain disciples, to gain devotees, are going to be very threatened by the awakening of the consciousness of the Rainbow People because the Rainbow People exist in every country, in every nation, in every land. In other words the Sun Dancers are going to be strong enough. The dark forces will be extremely threatened and they will use their power and their power exists in technology. We are going to see some of the most strong technological advances known to humanity occurring next year (1984) and these very technological advances are going to be a tremendous threat as well as a blessing to the survival of humanity. Now what is also a Heyoka (trickster) is that 1984 is also the year that we must establish balance and harmony between the light and the dark forces. It's going to be interesting and that's why we have this sense of urgency because it is getting short.

"Grace Walking Stick is the head seer and visionary of the Black Widow Society. She said there will be a major crisis to put us on the brink of nuclear war and the only thing that will stop it — is that the dark force is trying to create an artificial sun nuclear war — that we must exert the influence, the Sun Dancers, the Rainbow People, by smoking our pipes, of gathering together and of sharing our medicine for solar power, for world peace, and whatever else happens we MUST not give energy in protesting or being against something because if you take the amount of energy you spend marching, talking, writing letters against things and instead put an equal amount or double amount of energy with what you are for, we can change it. Example: Instead of protesting uranium, promote solar.

"If we get through this period, then there will be more teachers, and more teachings brought out to open format than has ever been seen on this planet in the first fifty thousand years. Because then we will reestablish contact in a very knowledgeable way with our ancestors from the stars. So mark that down because it will happen. The first wave will come from Pleiades and will be totally acknowledged and will be known by all the world powers. The second wave will come from Sirius.

"Ruby Morning Star was the head seer of the Crystal Skull Society. She said that in 1985 you will see a total change in the concept of what we call the United Nations. Instead of political opposition and struggle it will change names and become the new circle of law — the Eight Great Powers.

"When Tagashala and the enlightened teachers begin to open the veil of the crack between the worlds. We will see our memory circles. All Kivas and sacred power spots will come alive and be totally awakened. The inner room of the Great Pyramid will be opened. The Order of the Golden Dawn will have ceremonies there again for the first time in 20,000 years. The Temple of the Sun in Palenque will be refurbished, reawakened and ceremonies will begin. The old traditional ceremonies that are still applicable for today's world will be renewed. Many of the ceremonies that are so-called traditionalists, but are trying to keep us locked in the past and will not function today will fall. It will be hard for some of the people of the medicine societies because they don't know any other way. They're going to have to change or die. Many teachers who have been seen as great teachers, who have literally kept us in the dark as worshippers of the sacrament orders will physically die and go over because it's the only way they can find the light in 1986 and many teachers will be seen for what they were and they will be the farmers, the laborers, and the gas station attendants and they will be seen as the real teachers because the Tagashala will be fully awakened.

ENLIGHTENED TEACHERS

At this point, 144,000 Sun Dance enlightened teachers will totally awaken in their dream mind-bodies. They will begin to meet in their own feathered serpent or winged serpent wheels and become a major force of the light to help the rest of humanity to dance their dream awake. A Sun Dance teacher is any human being who has awakened, who has balanced their shields. Who has gained the dream mind-body and who honors all paths, all teachers, and always. I look for the day when I can sit down with my pipe and the Buddhists with theirs. You will see me sit down with my dagger and my Sufi drum, with my sword, my Shinto way, and my pipe, my Indian way. We're going to put our Soul out on the table and say "I love you all." This is a sacred dance. That's what 1987 is about. That'a a Sun Dancer. You cannot say that you have the only true way, for all ways are true. In 1987, 144,000 enlightened Souls will sit down in gathering together circles saying "Here it is Brothers and Sisters. Openly, totally — Come and receive it." A lot of these are going to be so-called common people and not the teachers you see up there now. On August 17, 1987 the various winged serpent wheels will begin to turn, to dance once again and when they do the Rainbow Lights will be seen in dreams all over the world and Those Rainbow Light dreams will help awaken the rest of humanity.

"We will sit in a new circle of law. Civil and social law will tumble. All civil and social laws by whatever governments will have to be in conformity with natural law or the people will not accept them and they will have the enlightenment necessary to reject the laws. Science will once again become metaphysics, will once again become magic. They will discover four laws that will help them jump from natural to magical law and transcend the time/space continuum which is the limitation of the age and once again we will begin to take our power and to work with rules and laws that are magical laws and cosmic laws.

"We will once again see the way to continue a new dream. We will be given the road map back to the stars and will see the star people come out of the illusion of their two-legged form and into their actual Great Sleeper-Dream form. And so you will see some very, very powerful, totally enlightened Masters and the second coming of the Christ spoken of in the Book of Relevations and it will be the awakening of a new circle, a new design of energy movement for humanity. Christ means a circle. So the second coming of the sacred circle is all enlightened humans dancing as one consciousness."

THE NEXT DECADE

Here is Swiftdeer's breakdown of the next decade in a year by year analysis of forthcoming events that are guaranteed to effect us all, rich or poor, young or old.

1990

"A powerful year and it's really hard for me to talk about it. I am a great dreamer but I don't know if I dream that large. We will see a real shift in planetary consciousness. Many of the enemies of the humans shall begin to drop away. In 1990 you will see the Twelve Sacred Driver Wheels of each of the Eight Powers stored and put together to create the figure 8 of infinity sign. And 1990 wil begin through the Feathered Serpent Medicine Wheels those groups of seventeen Great Sleeper Dreamers. The first migration to the next world will begin, leaving behind on this planet another world of enlightened humanity to join the many already on other planets throughout our universe. When you speak of this migration to other planets, are you speaking of a creation of a new race? Another dream, another dance, another series of dances in another dream in another world. What's the difference between this world and the new creation. It is those that go on ahead that are the pathfinders.

1991

"For those who stay here on Grandmother Earth, they will totally gain the light of the Great Light Wheel. That there will be one humanity, one planet composed of all the different ways of dancing in complete harmony in the great gathering together circle. In 1991 all the seeds will be planted.

1992

"The earth will have its true reality formed. It will join the sister-hood of planets, the Daughters of Copperwoman and it will create within itself all forms of all things in harmony with the everything.

1993

"We will see a whole new way of perfection. There will be plants on this Grandmother Earth that will give life and sustenance as never before seen. Starvation on the earth — all those things will be gone.

1994

"There will be total balance and harmony. All human beings will be balanced fives or enlightened fives — a six. And they will still be in their physical bodies.

1995

"The new race of humans will begin to design their new reality of life on this planet as they intended it to be when they came from the stars.

1996

"The second migration to the new world will occur leaving behind on Grandmother Earth those who are choosing to continue to hold the power on this planet within the space of all the Sacred Twelve. All of these people who choose to remain after the second migration will begin to establish this planet and use the collective unconscious to hold the power of this space in harmony with the Great Circle of Twelve, all the planets, and there is a whole lot I don't even know. There is more that I am not supposed to talk about yet.

1997

"The dream will be actualized and this planet will hold its space in the great Council of planets and become part of the Universal enlightened Brotherhood and Sisterhood of humanity because there is an organization that is intergalactic that is known as the Great International Brother and Sisterhood of Humanity and Keepers of the Light Circles. It's happened on many planets and it's expected to happen on a lot of other planets.

1998

"There will be a moment in 1998 when the population will be the population. The Circle of Law will hold the image of fast thought necessary to allow this planet to become a starship. (Is this fun? Not bad for a bunch of ignorant savages).

1999

"The Third migration will leave this planet for the other new world and this planet will now be a starship, a spaceship, have its design of energy movement guided by all of humanity that's living here because, see, it's been a starship all along floating around a central sun but not in harmony with sister planets.

2000

"In the year 2000 the Great Spirit will have left its seed and the egg of the everything here on this planet and it will create itself 20 times over at the speed of light and thus the prophecy ends as I have been given it by the Grandmother that I share with you now."

AND ATLANTIS SHALL RISE

"I feel that the lost continent of Atlantis will rise and it will be a place which man will want to colonize, for he will be looking for new frontiers to settle."
        Prediction by Ann Fasher
        Albany, N.Y. Psychic

Many of those involved in the casting off of the old system, and the development of a New Age, feel that we are not the first culture on earth to develop scientifically and technically. They contend that eons ago another "Super Civilization" existed on this planet and destroyed itself much as we are about to do. Psychics believe that the continent of Atlantis will rise in the End Times, more than likely just after the sinking of California's coast line. Already, underwater explorers have located the ruins of what some believe to be Atlantis in the waters off the coast of Bimini. Located in the area known as the Bermuda Triangle — where many planes and ships have mysteriously disappeared — the ruins remain a puzzle and strange laser-like beams of lights have been seen coming up from the ocean's bottom, indicating that some of the ancient machinery from Atlantis may still be in working order.

In an issue of the Solar Space Letter published by Robert Short, the channel tells us that there will be a recurrence of the Atlantean period. "There is a precedent for the incident we spoke about of, which could bring about that which you speak of as Armaggedon, in those areas, which are a part of those nations who are the sons and daughters of Ibrahim, or Abraham, in the early recorded eras upon your planet. Who were the descendants of those of the ancient land continent, which was DESTROYED BY WEAPONS WHICH NOW PREVAIL UPON YOUR PLANET, which was found in the MIDST OF THE WATERS, which parted, and it was rent assunder, and many were lost. These were called by you, the ANCIENT ATLANTEANS, or ALT-LANTEANS (old ones), which is referred to in that of your mythology, or legends of your past."

One belief has it that some of the Atlanteans escaped by building vast space ships and traveling to other stars. I am inclined to believe that some of the UFOs we see are piloted by former Atlanteans come back to assist the space people in removing us if and when necessary.

CHAPTER NINE

What The Prophets And Seers Predict

I f the events we have read about in the previous chapters must come to pass, then certainly we should be among those individuals who know exactly what precautions to take and where to go in order to be relatively safe and secure (at least until we have the opportunity to be "picked up" by our alien friends). In order to get a good overview of just this very subject, we have called upon a representative number of psychics and seers to give their opinions on this topic, based upon strong clairvoyance. The first such person we hear from is Francie Steiger of Phoenix, Arizona.

AN IMPORTANT VISION
On May 22, 1979, Francie was en-route to San Juan, Puerto Rico. During the flight from New York to the islands, she had a vision which instructed her to warn those people who live in coastal regions that these locations would become dangerous during the approaching time of transition.

Francie has spoken distinctly of the various changes that are to take place: "Those who live on the coastal regions of all countries

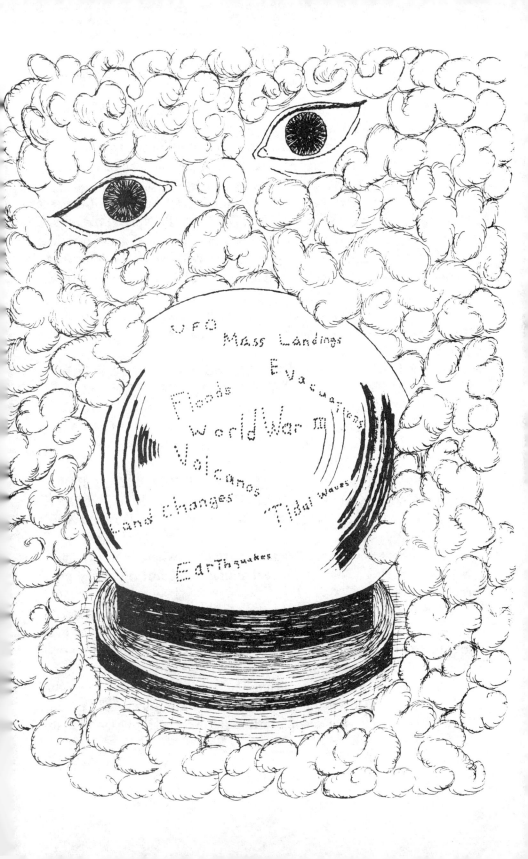

will be in danger during the time of transition, which will accelerate in the 1980s.

"The entire Earth will experience many disasters — quakes, floods, splittings, and famine. An inner shift of energies, of polarities, will occur, shaking our very foundation. Those who seek to live by the Spirit must be strong in the years which lie ahead. All will be affected by these many catastrophes in varying degrees."

The changes that she saw happening took the form of a great three-pronged split that extended down from the North Pole region.

"In the manner of a three-taloned claw, this will gravely affect the Earth's crust and will cause considerable devastation. This three-taloned claw will encompass half of the world, and will indicate areas of great tension and stress."

Francie, in her vision, saw the exact location of the three talons and the effect — a far reaching one — that they will have on the planet.

- THE FIRST TALON WILL CROSS DIAGONALLY, DOWN-WARD OVER THE EASTERN REGION OF THE SOVIET UNION, THEN LOWER INTO EASTERN CHINA.
- THE SECOND TALON WILL STRETCH DIAGONALLY DOWNWARD ACROSS CENTRAL CANADA AND INTO MID-CALIFORNIA.
- THE THIRD TALON WILL CROSS CENTRAL GREEN-LAND, FROM NORTHWEST TO EAST, MOVE DOWN-WARD INTO THE MEDITERRANEAN AND INTO NOR-THERN AFRICA.

"These are the places," Francie contends, "where major tensions will exist during the coming electromagnetic shifting of the polar regions.

"Areas on either side of the three gripping talons will be affected," she adds, "but all land near the coastal regions will suffer to an even greater degree with quakes, floods, great winds, and climatical changes. Those areas further inland will be the least afflicted.

"The time of great devastation has occurred on Earth twice before. On the first occasion, there were only animals on the planet. On the second occasion, people suffered the catastrophes, and many

earlier cultures and civilizations were destroyed. Francie's chanı.
stated during this vision that, "These great devastations are vibrа
tional, accumulative events which are natural to this planet. No one
knows the exact time the fast-approaching devastation will begin,
but it will be soon, quite likely before 1999."

Francie was told that in order to discover the "safe" places during the coming cataclysms, one must first "feel" and meditate upon
those areas which are the strongest. When choosing a place to live,
one must select a solid area that can withstand great strain.

"Feel those areas which emanate the *least* vibrations," Francie
advised. "Study the topography of all regions and ascertain those
which are the driest. Areas near bodies of water of any major pro-
portion are in danger. Water in vast amounts will shift, take different courses, different directions, and be jarred from present bound-
aries. The amount of miles inland which will be considered a safe
area will depend upon the size of the body of water it is near.

"Even in the driest of areas, far from water, the present emanations existing suggest splittings, shiftings, settlings, and major cave-
ins. These ground shifts will occur not only in regions near the three-
pronged strain, but in particular areas that were once seabeds, where
underground caverns now exist. These regions will not be able to
withstand the shaking, the shifting and the strain."

Francie maintains that the safest regions will likely be the "desert
regions — as long as one takes into consideration those areas which
are presently desert, but are dangerous due to their proximity to
large bodies of water."

According to the information channeled through Francie the
following areas are to be sought out as the safest regions on the
planet:

- MAJOR PARTS OF ARIZONA.
- THE SOUTHERN PART OF COLORADO.
- THE LARGE, WESTERN AREA OF NEW MEXICO, AND
  THE NORTHERN REGION OF MEXICO.
- INLAND AUSTRALIA WILL BE SAFE, AS IS MID-
  ARABIA, THE SOUTHWEST SOVIET UNION, AND THE
  DRIEST REGION OF NORTHWEST CHINA.

During the course of her vision, Francie was instructed to tell, "You, who are Star People, to permit your 'mark on the forehead,' the so-called 'Third Eye,' to lead you to safety. As you keep in mind the regions above, meditate upon the area of thought that feels safe to you. You are aware that the dangerous emanations and regions do exist. Your inner guidance will help you make your final decision in ascertaining your safest place.

Concludes Francie: "All people of Spirit must be ready to share their energies during this time. The Star People's capacity to love will be greater, as they observe the birth throes of a New World of higher vibrational frequencies. Love must be the guiding force in all that we undertake. The next two decades will be among the most important that humankind has ever faced. The entire species is about to face its moment of decision."

AND CALIFORNIA SHALL FALL INTO THE SEA

To a person, all the psychics we have discussed this matter with, seem convinced that California's days are numbered, that it shall fall into the sea. Most psychics are relatively certain that the slippage of the West Coast will be among the first of the truly great catastrophies, and will usher in many of the other traumatic events we have unlocked the seal of knowledge on.

Helen Cassimos is not a "professional" when it comes to seeing into the future. But, once or twice during her life she has had what she believes are definite clairvoyant experiences which allowed her to project her mind to a date months or even years from the present. "It all started one hot summer night," the talented photographer explained. "It was probably around 4 A.M. and I was still tossing and turning in bed trying to get to sleep. Before I realized what was happening I found myself standing atop a mountain from where I could see the shores of California for miles. The winds were sending the sea water a half mile into the air. Suddenly, the earth trembled, the ground shook with a mighty force and I could see the far-off villages and towns glowing, as fires blazed out of control.

"I could see heavily populated areas caving-in and the ground just seemed to swell and buckle. Cars moving along the main streets of

Los Angeles and San Francisco were swallowed up as the earth shifted to and fro.

"In a matter of minutes portions of California were slipping off into the sea and the screams of a million persons filled the air. I then came to, in a cold sweat, only to realize that what I had just had was a psychic impression of what was to come — a prophecy of a day not too far away when there would be mighty earth changes."

Introduced earlier in this book, we should remind you that Pauline Sharpe is a 48-year-old channel who uses the spiritual name of Yolanda in her work as co-director of the Mark-Age MetaCenter, an organization dedicated to preparing our planet for the much discussed "Golden Age," slated to transpire after the end of the "Harvest Period," the age when "all error will be swept from the earth and from the minds of those men who would remain as they are now."

Yolanda has received many visions as they relate to the End Times. She accompanies this deed by relaxing her body and opening her inner eyes. "With the inner eye I visualize a darkness, such as a room or a screen. Then I allow the High Self to project ideas, so to speak, into that darkness or void across that screen. When such ideas are given I try to cling to them, allowing them to develop. Sometimes I can achieve this only for a few minutes, but often for hours." Yolanda admittedly owes a great deal to her space contacts. "The Space Brothers are here to teach us there is a federation of planets," she states. "I act as a spokesman for them and it is my job to teach and help awaken our spirits to rise to higher levels of awareness." Yolanda's primary contact is a space being named Zumah who transmits messages from a mothership high above the surface of the earth. More than any other group of individual, Yolanda and her co-worker Mark, have been able to pinpoint specific changes in our planet's crust that may cause land masses to sink and to rise from the depths of the ocean.

These are some of the predictions Yolanda has given out, more-or-less on a state-by-state basis; along with the date each vision took place.

WASHINGTON AND OREGON

In the valleys between the Cascade and the Bitterfoot Mountains, the Blue and the Wallowa Mountains, and in the valleys between central and northeastern Oregon there is a sense of greed, selfishness, lack of cooperation; even snobbishness is expressed in these Umatilli and Yakima Valley regions. There is lushness and abundance, an obvious material success through the land in these fruit and wheat bowls. The elements have been generous here, but man has hoarded and has exploited his fellow-man. Since love, thanks and humility are not felt and given freely, it shall be forced through nature.

CALIFORNIA

San Francisco itself will experience severe earthquakes during the next ten years, but it is not likely that it will suffer irreparable damage. Between Vallejo and the Golden Gate Bridge there will be irretrievable losses, but the area south of that will survive the stresses better than is presently anticipated.

The gradual rising of the continent of Lemuria in the Pacific will change the ocean currents between southern Washington and central California. This activity will create a more bay-like temperament in the waters and will change the weather conditions radically for this western coast, thereby also altering other conditions that depend on the weather. For example, the fog and rainy atmosphere of San Francisco area will clear, and the weather there will be much milder, by ten or twenty degrees.

Tidal waves will result, sweeping across the continent to the Rockies. But they will not cover the entire coastal region; only small sections will be troubled.

Sacramento may well become one of the most important capital cities in the United States, since California may be the most significant state in the union. After some land shifts, new gold pockets will be opened.

The Santa Monica Mountains from Sherman Oaks to Universal City are to be radically changed, flattened by erosion and unprecedented storms.

The area of California that will be most dangerous is between the San Bernardino National Forest and the Santa Ana Mountains and includes the cities of Riverside, Palm Springs and Corona. A network of connecting underground tunnels will experience a series of explosions, such as caused by underground volcanoes, which eventually will destroy the foundation or crust support in this region. It will result in the land caving in due to erosion, heat and tremors.

It is interesting to take note of the fact that Yolanda's predictions are at least similar in part to the channeled messages received through Thedra, a West Coast prophet who claims a "direct link" with the Space Brothers. "They are to be the ones who awaken to find their beds soaked wth the waters of the Pacific, and the place shall be from Seattle to the coast of Chile whereupon the great caps shall roll back unto the Rocky Mountains . . . Furthermore, the land will be as drenched though not as sunken. The great places of the coast of the Pacific will be no more."

Yolanda's channels repeatedly spoke to her of widespread disasters that would cause havoc to rain on the earth. "And there shall be great ocean liners, liners which shall travel within its waters, which shall be propelled by solar energy of the next age, and with this they shall be unable to travel east or west or from west to east, through what is now the Atlantic Ocean, for it shall have a mountain range which has been thrown up from the bottom of the Atlantic, and it shall be extended into the air to the altitude of 10,000 feet. And it shall be as the Sittur of old, for it was the Light of the world that this land once took her place in the sun. And she went down amid a great shock and a great wave: and it shall be that she shall come up the same way as she went down."

This seems to be a description of the rising of Atlantis which we reviewed a few pages back. All of these events tie in and are likely to occur at roughly the same time, though we do not know the exact day — no one does!

AND THERE SHALL COME A GREAT TIDAL WAVE

Earlier, we printed a special report by researcher Jon Singer on the increase in earthquakes up and down the entire east coast, and how they are far more severe than any others recorded in the last one hundred years or more. The predictions of the psychics all add up to the fact that these quakes will be increasing both in frequency and in magnitude, and they will be joined by other cataclysmic events.

Barbara Hudson the UFO channel we talked about previously in chapter seven, has had a total of eight or nine visions of New York City being destroyed.

Drawing by Barbara Hudson

"Each time I saw New York being hit by a gigantic tidal wave," Barbara states. "In one vision, I saw myself inside Riverside Church somewhere high up — like in a tower. The only furnishings in the room I was in were a huge cross, a desk and a chair." Through a nearby archway window, Barbara described to me how water seemed to be rising in every direction, covering most of the buildings in the vicinity. "Suddenly, the floor I was standing on gave way, and I was positioned on a ledge looking down several hundred feet into the body of the Church." Here, too, the water was rising, and it seemed that the dark green liquid would reach her in a matter of moments. At this point the vision faded.

On another occasion, while giving medical treatment to a patient in St. Luke's Hospital, at Amsterdam Avenue and 114th Street, where she was an orderly, Barbara described how she had chanced to glance out the hospital window, since the room seemed to be obstructed by a strange color coming from somewhere outside.

"I noticed that the sun looked funny — almost orange-yellow in color — with a strange fog that seemed to hover above the skyline. I then heard a rumble and saw water rolling over the city in every direction. Instead of one large tidal wave, the sky looked like an ocean of white-capped waves."

Between nearby Morningside Park and St. Luke's Hospital, Barbara explained, the street split, leaving a wide valley where seconds before hundreds of cars had been moving on it. "At that, I looked back toward my patient for a brief moment and when I turned back the scene below was once again normal."

Barbara Hudson's most frightening experience, however, happened even more recently. She walked over to the kitchen window near where I was seated and looked out through the storm screen. "I was standing by this window and noticed that the sky and sun looked as it had done previously during my visions. I then saw what appeared to be a long grey line above the buildings, which seemed to be moving toward my apartment building."

Initially, Barbara thought this grey line was a strange formation of clouds. "Then I noticed that the air was full of a deafening roar and the buildings were snapping in two as the 'cloud' passed over. As the grey line approached uptown I could see that this line was in reality a huge tidal wave." It hit Riverside Church, Barbara told me as I listened attentively to her story. The force of the impact was so great that the entire foundation crumbled to the ground.

"Seeing this, I grabbed my young daughter by the arm," realizing the tidal wave would soon reach them, "and ran into the hall in an attempt to get to the roof. As I reached the stairway, I noticed that water had already began to pour in through the skylight and was filling up the stairwell and would reach our position soon.

"I noticed also that the water was seeping under the closed roof door. Frightened I might be swept down the stairs by the force of the raging tide, I opened the door only a crack at first. Seeing that it was only a few inches deep, I pulled the door completely open and carried my daughter to the roof."

Once there, Barbara proceeded to climb onto a vent-type structure which rose an additional three or four feet from the rooftop. But even here the deadly water continued to rise. She stood at the kitchen window, only a few feet away from me, and continued with her frightening vision. "Looking out over the city, I could see an identical situation, with only a few of the really tall buildings left uncovered. For those structures which had not been crushed by the force of the tidal wave itself were now completely covered by the still rising water."

When Barbara came out of her altered state the first thing she remembered is how vivid the vision had been. "I remember saying when I came around, 'Oh, my God, I wish that this would never happen,' but I know it will, sometime in my lifetime."

THE END TIME VISIONS OF ANTHONY AND LYNN VOLPE

I was first introduced to Anthony and Lynn Volpe in Pittsburgh, Pennsylvania, where I had organized an all day conference on the UFO enigma. During a break in the proceedings they came forward to tell me they believed in UFOs and had actually made contact with amphibian beings from the constellation of Pegasus. The Ivyland, Pennsylvania couple say that they have put together musical vibrations and recorded it on cassette tape and actually brought in a UFO during 1977, much like the scientists in Close Encounters of the Third Kind attempted to do. "This music appears to have magical qualities about it," the heads of a local UFO group maintain, adding, that if they get permission from "our space friends," they may play the tape at a future seminar of mine and attempt to bring in a UFO, "or some sort of manifestation."

Regarding End Time prophecies the Volpe's say that the east coast will be flooded out before too many years have passed.

Here is Lynn's account of her various experiences:

"For the past seven years I have had visionary dreams of the flooding out of the eastern seaboard. The Atlantic Ocean would be seen moving in over the coastal areas rapidly and steadily. In my vision my house was uprooted and in astral travel, I was able to look down over the east coast, and it looked like the middle of the Atlantic. This flooding out will take place over a two year period and will also include the midwestern section of the country, almost as far as the Mississippi River, Illinois and Indiana.

"In one vision I saw many small fissures in the earth, opening up along the east coast, pulling apart the land and causing water to erupt from these openings. These are 'mini fault lines' of which scientists know nothing.

"Another time, Trenton, New Jersey was being flooded out. People in the city were going up to the top of high rise buildings. There was a book there where people were checking to see if their name had been entered. This was called 'Mary's Book of Records.'

"These tidal waves and small cracks were being aggravated by constant atomic explosions. This 'baptism' of the east coast will be like a cleansing and redemption of the earth which will help people toward a greater awakening of universal brotherhood."

The visions of the Volpe's are quite stimulating to our mind, as they confirm what we have learned from other sources. Anthony recently found himself on board a space ship looking down at the earth as great changes were taking place. "It was as if I belonged there, as sort of a 'dual existence' (author's note: Is this another possible example of 'Blends' or 'Star People' experiencing EndTime events?). I looked down through a viewing port which was like a window in the floor and saw the earth, which appeared as large as a grapefruit at arms length. It was my task to record what I was about to see, as I knew something important was to transpire at that moment; namely, changes within the earth's structure. Suddenly, the earth expanded as if it were a balloon being filled with air. It expanded about twenty per cent and then returned to its normal size. While in the expanded state, the topographical features were all disturbed. However, when the earth 'regrouped itself' or returned to its normal size, the surface was once again normal. As all this was taking place, I was busy recording the events from on board the space craft."

Frankly, I'm intrigued about Lynn Volpe's vision involving constant atomic explosions along the east coast which would aggravate the already horrifying series of events caused by earth tremors. One of the psychics Robert Short has worked with says that in a trip to the future he witnessed similar events. In Oak Ridge, Chattanooga, Knoxville (Tennessee) six nuclear reactors and power plants went off almost simultaneously. The earthquakes in this area just broke the reactors apart . . . Its now a desert there." Food for thought, but not very pleasant tasting, indeed!

Here are just a few of Yolanda's predictions involving the states along the east coast, as dispensed by her group known as Mark Age:

FLORIDA AND GEORGIA

In the time of great land upheavals, southern Georgia (between Albany and Eastman) to central Florida will remain virtually intact and will be a reservoir for supplies, such as food and cotton, and would be an aid in regrowth and redevelopment for other areas which are to be changed. This area in central Georgia is the heart of a conservation belt and this is the reason light workers, groups and sanctuaries have been attracted to it.

Yolanda and Mark from the Mark Age Foundation

NORTH CAROLINA AND TENNESSEE

At the southernmost tip of the Blue Ridge Mountains in North Carolina, just before reaching the Smoky Mountains (which are predominantly in Tennessee), I received that this area was to be changed. The mountains will shift from north of Atlanta, Georgia, to Asheville, North Carolina, and including Knoxville, Tennessee, to Oak Ridge where the Atomic Energy Commission is based.

VIRGINIA

From Danville to Virginia Beach the earthquake is invigorating and healthy. This has been noticeable in the past, and it continues to be vigorous. In Norfolk a projection of power through us for peace, love and brotherhood was anchored to help avert racial and industrial disturbance. This area must act as a levering agent in future natural upheavals. Richmond, the capital of Virginia, has certain positive and energetic forces due to general vigor of the entire state of awareness.

WASHINGTON, D.C.

The atmosphere in the nation's capital and its outlying districts is very disturbing. There is confusion and hustle without spiritual significance, roads which are more a maze than routes for transportation. There is an ominous feeling regarding the safety of this city ... There will be a collapse in Washington, some form of tragedy, some cataclysm; which does not refer necessarily to natural holocaust, but to that realm of human thoughts and thus of human acts.

As you can tell many sections will be unsafe and these are the places that should be kept away from once the signs have begun to appear all around us. However, according to Yolanda and Mark Age there will be places to go. These are some of the suggested regions:

TEXAS

Texas functions as a balance wheel ... Its mission is to demonstrate balance of opportunity, or utilizations of mineral, vegetable and animal life. In these days of international and interplanetary interests it is unlikely that Texans will lose sight of the spiritual purpose behind their state's function. And with balance and integrity, health and wholeness in its citizens, it can be the center and pride of all the American people.

COLORADO

The Rockies will protect much of the central continent from the forthcoming Pacific Ocean tidal waves. Water may immerse the lower ranges, but not much will spill over as could spoil Denver or other cities on the eastern slopes. From the Rockies to the Mississippi River will be the safest areas from which to rebuild the nation. Much of this region will remain unspoiled, with vast sections mentally and physically unpolluted by man.

PENNSYLVANIA

The Allegheny Mountains are embedded with the feelings of grace, beauty, stability and security. The elements themselves seemed to reassure us, as we motored through. No matter what catastrophes occur in the impending earth changes ahead, here you will be safe, protected and productive.

ILLINOIS

This state is what we call the heart center of a new civilization. For this reason it has to be kept pure and uncontaminated. The area is favorable to much planting. The development of Lostant, Illinois, approximately forty miles north of Bloomington, may explode due to a mineral discovery, probably oil.

We would be amiss to claim that it is within the scope of this book to print even a small per cent of the prophecies that have come through Yolanda. We have had to "water down" (and please excuse the pun) much of that which has been received by this particular channel. Should interest exist to obtain further details not covered here we know you would be welcome to write to Mark Age Associates at 327 N.E. 20th Terrace, Miami, Florida 33137.

THE TIME HAS ARRIVED TO TAKE PRECAUTIONS

With earthquakes due to breakout on a wide scale in the very near future, now is the time to start taking precautions that will enable you to weather the storm. One creative individual who is aware of the End Times prophecies is Joe Campbell of Roseland, VA, a former news anchorman with the Mutual Broadcasting Systems, a radio network with over 150 affiliate stations nationwide. Recently retired from his job as a science correspondent, Joe has started a unique group in the Blue Ridge Mountains of Virginia. Known as "Kenton — Turning Earth Group," it is his goal to supply so-called "Doomsday Crafts" to the public. "If these events we have heard about start happening in 1982 or thereabouts, people will need a craft built specifically to meet such a catastrophe in order to survive in certain areas." Joe has recently completed a prototype of such a craft. The imposing structure is a 22-foot sphere made from interlocking triangles of wood, braced with steel bars with cement. The cement is weighted toward the bottom, so that it will float without overturning.

Weighing 16 tons and valued at $20,000 the craft has two interior decks, one with bunks, galley, bathroom and storage holds, the other the main living area. A "crow's nest" at the top level has 19 scientific instruments — everything from a radioactivity meter to a complete weather station. A few feet above the water line, the ship is rimmed with 30 portholes, plus one large hexagonal window. It will have no means of propulsion other than the movement of the ocean current.

"You could build one on the San Andreas Fault, and if an earthquake struck, you'd soon be floating safely in the Pacific," notes Campbell. For those who cannot afford having such a craft made to order, Joe plans to make available do-it-yourself kits which will give easy-to-read instructions. "This may all seem far-fetched to some people," admits the former newsman, "but in the days ahead I think people will be thankful that such a device exists and can provide them with a degree of safety and comfort they might not be able to enjoy otherwise."

It is indeed interesting to discover that the idea of this being the

Dieu se sert icy de ma bouche
Pour t'anoncer la verité
Si ma prediction te touche
Rends grace à sa Divinité

Nostradamus is considered to be the most accurate seer who ever lived. Many of his predictions made hundreds of years ago are strikingly similar to what has been forecast by others, including famed "Sleeping Prophet," Edgar Cayce.

start of the End Times has passed beyond the involvement of psychics and UFO channels, and has now penetrated into other echelons of society. That gentlemen the likes and caliber of Joe Campbell should devote their time and energy to this field, is a strong indication that we should take these warnings more seriously.

ALIGNMENT OF THE PLANETS

Back a decade ago there was a tremendous uproar in the so-called "Jupiter Effect" which called for all the planets in the solar system to "line up" in space. For the most part the scientific community ridiculed the very idea that such a conjunction could have a noticeable effect on Earth. On the other hand a number of psychics and a community of "New Agers" who in general tend to accept the belief that the planets do play a part in our lives, strongly stated that this alignment would cause many negative influences including earthquakes, bad weather and volcanic eruptions.

As the media is prone to do, newspapers and TV picked up on this story and produced wild speculation in a very sensationalistic manner in order to grab headlines. Without having access to all the facts the press picked up on the date March 10th, 1982 and broadcast the message that everyone who believed in the occult thought the world was going to end sometime around high noon. Never once did they bother to interview anyone who might have an inkling of the real situation — they expected that their blanket statements would cause a good laugh among members of their audience who obviously are not aware of the true facts on this matter.

The truth is that not one psychic ever predicted DOOMSDAY was coming on March 10th. In fact, on March 10th only five planets were in the same approximate portion of the heavens, the other planets left to join them later in the year.

"We've always talked about an overall — a prolonged — affect," notes Thelma Terrell of Ashtar Command.

"Remember," Thelma points out, "a lot of changes that have been predicted will be on a spiritual level and not so much on the physical plane."

However, this is not to say that "NOTHING" did happen around the March 10th deadline for the end of the world.

As predicted, we had the worst winter recorded in this century. This included 45-foot deep snow drifts in California, floods in the central portions of the U.S., a tidal wave which pounded the South Sea island kingdom of Tonga (drowning at least two children as 172 mile per hour winds from a cyclone injured hundreds more and tossed homes the length of a football field), and a blizzard that rocked the mid-west and east coast the week of Easter, postponing Spring till well into April. In addition, several earthquakes shook the floor of Mount St. Helen in Oregon sending lava and volcanic dust into the atmosphere. Residents of Mexico were hit even harder when a volcano believed to be inactive exploded killing ten people who tried to seek refuge inside a church.

But perhaps the most important aspect of the March conjunction, was the appearance of a "mysterious cloud" that circled the Northern Hemisphere as far south as Costa Rica and as far north as Wyoming. Scientists had to admit that they could not come up with a quick explanation for the 10 mile high "cloud" which made for some colorful twilights wherever it was seen.

"This cloud was most definitely a mother ship," insists UFO RE-VIEW subscriber Victoria Bloom of St. Charles, Missouri. "It is an old and well established fact that 'They' comest in a cloud," apparently referring to Biblical texts. "It's a wonder the scientists don't say it is *swamp gas*," Victoria jokes, but adds in a serious tone, "We will be hearing more about this thru our UFO channels."

Because of wide spread interest in End Times predictions, we have included a list of the events forecast by some of the most outstanding ˙ sensitives of our time. We have only to keep an open mind and watch the heavens in the coming months for "Signs and Wonders" which proclaim that a "Golden Age" is coming.

IRENE HUGHES

Irene Hughes is perhaps the top psychic and medium operating out of the mid-west. She is a professional astrologer and a journalist with 15 awards to her credit. Irene's syndicated radio program is aired over 40 stations each week, and has written several books on parapsychology including one with Brad Steiger titled PSYCHIC SUFARRY. In addition to her lectures and classes which she teaches, Irene is often called upon by police departments in criminal matters. (Irene F. Hughes Ltd., 500 North Avenue, Chicago, IL 60611).

"I began talking about the turbulent 1980s and 90s as far back as 1959. I had predicted that there would be terrible earthquakes throughout the year 2046, with some of the worst ones happening in California.

"Incredible earth changes will occur, such as volcanoes erupting in Hawaii, and some of the Hawaiian Islands disappearing. There will be tremendous flooding and tidal waves in that area.

"There will be tremendous earth changes connected with New York City, as I do feel that because of perhaps atomic war, that it will totally disappear and because of tremendous earthquakes, that are going to happen in the state of New York.

"California won't sink into the Pacific, but I do feel that it will split in two and that an earthquake will rip it asunder, probably between 1986 and 1996.

"Organized religion will totally fall — that is the organizational and orthodoxy part of it. The fact that there is a presence that we call God will be more evident than ever and man will discover as it was told him originally, but which has been denied him, the fact that God is within.

"UFOs will be no longer a mystery and we will find that a number of nations have been involved in creating such space ships that can actually fly. We will also discover that indeed, ships of this nature were discovered in the Valley of the Moon and that we will find that ancient civilizations did use such ships in their travel. We will find that they were made billions of years ago and didn't deteriorate in the interplanetary space just as our space ships will not for billions of years, and some other civilization in the future will find them floating down. We will have space stations going extremely well in the late 1990s and in the year 2001 or 2003. The first child will probably be born in a space station near Mars.

"There will, indeed, be great droughts and shortages of food all over the world, so that our diets will change and the preservation through dehydration of foods and the new methods of combining vitamins and nutrients for our bodies will come about.

"New planets will be discovered near the Constellation Taurus, and asteroids will be closer to the earth than ever before. We will find that in 1986, when Haley's Comet returns, that the indications are its extreme closeness to our planet, and that tremendous meteorites will fall before its trip is over.

"The aging process will find tremendous breakthroughs so that man will look younger and find that cells can be rebuilt within the brain and in other areas of the body to prevent us from growing older.

"Kindness towards one another will be enhanced and a great love for one another will come about, but in a different way. There will not be any one world government nor any one world religion.

"Incredible weather will continue, so, as I predicted as long ago as 1959, that we would see the beginnings of an ice age in various areas of the U.S. We will have horrendous electrical storms in this area and in the Northwest and Southwest and we will have some unbelievable storms in the coming years as they become more electrical."

BILL COX

Famed pyramidologist Bill Cox got out his dowsing equipment when he heard we wanted a reading as to what changes were going to take place on this planet.

"I've done some dowsing on this and I've found that the moon has a tremendous effect on our planet — a great pulling and releasing power. There is definitely a pushing that comes from the other planets in space, and I think the conjunction of the planets on one side of the earth will be felt in years to come.

"Actually, I became interested in this years ago because of the predictions that California would one day sink into the sea due to a major earthquake. There is no question that we do have the St. Andreas Fault which is 100 million years or more old. However, I don't see the state splitting in two like some psychics have forecast. If the St. Andreas Fault were going to crack it has had an awful long time to do so.

"However, there is a great deal of documented information to support the idea that the earth is about to undergo a transformation through a series of devastating upheavals, perhaps brought about because of certain planetary influences. Some of this evidence goes back to the discovery of the planet Uranius in 1781. The best investigation on this was done by a geo-physisist from the University of Munich. He wrote a paper in 1953 which told of his findings showing that there were a number of earthquakes that coincided with planetary movements, particularly in relation to Uranius. Apparently; there were some 134 earthquakes when this planet was in a certain position in the heavens.

"I believe that the earth probably shows its reaction to planetary bodies over prolonged periods, maybe even coinciding with an increase in sunspots as well.

"We know that the moon has pronounced effects on bodies of water, but so do earth tides. My mentor and teacher, the late Verne L. Cameron, found that in some places the earth was actually pulled out of its curve from two to three feet by tides of the moon in places where the earth was unstable.

"Though I have been warned to leave Calif. I am still here. I tend to believe it may be through a series of upheavals that the state will lose some of its land to the ocean. But the positive thoughtforms sent out by people could have an effect on this. It is believed by some of the UFO contactees that the space people are continually working to relieve the stress on the earth's crust."

LU.AH.MAH

Lu.Ah.Mah is an El Paso, Texas channel who received messages on a regular basis from those identifying themselves as members of the "celestial realms," as well as "our brothers and sisters from beyond the stars." Beings from the planet Mars, Saturn and Jupiter communicate on a regular basis. "It is my understanding that these cosmic communicators live in the sixth, seventh, eighth, and upwards dimensions; therefore they are visible to us only by choice."

Lu.Ah.Mah is the head of the Church of Universal Love located at 8034 Lowd, El Paso, TX 79907.

"In their communiques, the Cosmic and Space Masters continuously stress the primary importance of the spiritual changes which are an integral part of the stepped-up vibrations now in effect upon our earth. 'Pressure' is the key word. These pressures will be distinguishable on all levels, physical, mental, emotional, and spiritual, affecting first the inhabitants of our planet and then spilling over into the environment.

"Briefly, the severity of physical plane earthquakes will depend upon the disposition of each individual's own personal 'earthquakes.' It will be a time for the resurrecting of problems which have not been met head on and handled by my people and nations. The fall-out of these pressures will encompass problems involving relationships with people, groups of people, economics, and health on both the personal and national-international levels. Nationally and world-wide, relationships with people, other nations, religion, and military matters will not be put off any longer.

"The law of probability is now printing out some definite warning signs as far as earthquakes in our western coastal states are concerned. Yet with the help of our Space Friends and the Light Workers upon this planet, that which is predicted would appear to be minor — unless there is a significant buildup of world negativity. All earth changes will serve as a herald or harbinger for that which is to come, a "sneak perview," if you will for the remainder of the century.

"Severe and unseasonable weather will continue to be in the news. Some infringement of seawater upon coastal areas is seen, but these are mild compared to that which will occur later in the decade. Tuning into the vibrations of both San Francisco and San Diego, a great massing of higher vibrations seems to have formed protective cones of light. But there does seem to be some news-worthy activity in the Sacramento area.

"Continuing small quakes in unusual areas such as the south and midwest also are being reflected upon the screen of the future. Food shortages will become more critical in some parts of the world with

Nuclear power plants are a potential danger as when earthquakes strike they could be damaged and send radioactive particles into the air.

the likelihood that some items may become temporarily unavailable on U.S. market shelves. Land rising in Bimini should become more apparent. Possibility of topographical and civil upheavals are a strong bet in Turkey/Italy or the Middle East.

"This testing time should be viewed as a time of opportunity, for pressure can also be utilized as an impetus and a lever to increase awareness in a much shorter period of time. All times of stress have the tendency to accelerate wisdom, understanding, and truth for those who are receptive. The bridegroom of the New Age beckons; it is time for us to work together trimming our wicks with love and filling our lamps with the Higher Light . . . THERE IS NO ALTERNATIVE."

* * *

And what might the ultimate disaster be shortly before the period of "cleansing" comes about. The next chapter, dear reader, will provide many clues to our study of prophecy.

CHAPTER TEN

The Ultimate Disaster
And The Awakening

The ultimate disaster say many seers, may be a polar shift in which our entire planet would flip end over end in space. The result would be upheaval the likes of which we can only imagine. If the earth were to slip from its current axis, the polar ice caps could end up in the tropical zone, and our warm climates would turn suddenly cold.

Ruth Montgomery, Edgar Cayce, Paul Solomon, Nostradamus, Helena Blavatsky and the Hopi Indians all predict that the Earth will flip on its axis. Most envision this as happening shortly — usually around the year 2,000. Writer and researcher Dorothy Starr of San Diego has become a spokesperson on the subject. This is how she outlines the potentially catastrophic situation.

"The Antarctic Ice Cap is enormous. It would cover the United States and most of Canada. Ice is two miles high at the Pole. Unless the growth is controlled it will tip over the earth causing a world flood. Hugh Auchincloss Brown, an engineer explains in CATACLYSMS OF THE EARTH how this will be done.

"The earth, says the Engineer, is stabilized and held to its Axis of

Figure (North, South Poles) by the centrifugal force of the equatorial bulge. The gyroscopic energy of the rotating bulge steadies the globe and keeps it from rolling haphazardly. "The earth thus functions in the manner of a flywheel."

"The wobble of the earth results in a wandering of the Pole of Figure, the center of gyration of the polar ice caps. The linear speed of the ice caps increases at about 6.28 times their distance from the Axis of Spin; the total energy of motion and the "throw" of centrifugal force of the ice caps both increase proportionally with the weight of the ice mass that is off-center and at a rate which is the square of its velocity. The speed of travel is a function both of the rotation and the wobble of the earth. As the ice cap grows the wobble of the earth gives it a greater and greater linear motion which shows in an increased centrifugal force, and this tends to provide greater inertia until the stabilizing effect of the earth bulge is overcome and the earth rolls sideways to its direction of rotation. This flings the poles toward the equator and equator lands toward the poles.

"Rhinoceroses have been found in the permanently frozen ground of the Arctic regions, showing that tropical lands were flung poleward. Mammouths ar found in upright position with grass in their mouths and stomachs. They were suddenly killed by the tipping earth rushing their grazing lands to the Arctic. Some have broken bones as if the terrible winds of the tip-over had tossed them about then buried them under the debris where they quickly froze in their new cold climate. There they remained thousands of years to tell us today the story of the earth's tipping.

"Great loads of bones of horses, cattle, camels and other animals were found in the frozen tundra of Siberia. How did they get there if the earth did not roll their grazing lands poleward. Surely the frozen tundra could not supply vegetation to feed such hordes.

"Mr. Brown gives us much more evidence from fossils, sea life, legends and archaeology of the former tip-overs or "careens" of the earth.

"There is palemagnetic evidence. Rocks show the periodic reversal of earth's geomagnetic field. See DEBATE ABOUT THE

EARTH (Hitoshi Takeuchi, Seiya Uyeda and Hiroo Kanamori) pp. 149-51. Also the *U.S. Geological Survey Report* in *SCIENCE* 144, 1964 pp. 1537-43, titled, *Reversals of the Earth's Magnetic Field,* (R.R. Doell, A. Cox). From these magnetic reversals north was once south, it seems. Well, the old poles DO get around! For years Mr. Brown has said the poles have moved over the earth; now we find the rocks agree with him.

IS THE ICE CAP REALLY GROWING?

"THE POLAR ICE CAPS (A. Bauer, C. Lorius) 1964 says the volume of ice IS increasing annually enough to lower the sea level and that the sea level increase may be due to the expansion of water as a result of higher ocean temperatures. THE DYNAMICS OF THE ANTARCTIC ICE COVER (Markov, K.K.) 1962, says the Antarctic Ice Sheet has grown. Dr. P.A. Shumsky reported at the Symposium in Helsinki, 1960, that the South Polar Ice Cap grows at the rate of 293 cubic miles of ice a year. (See Mr. Brown's News Release.) Dr. Malcolm Mellors of Australia corroborated the Cap's growth.

"Not all glaciologists agree on the Cap's growth, but if just one has evidence of growth that should cause investigation."

Likewise, John White, a Cheshire, Connecticut resident, and a veteran researcher in the fields of parascience and consciousness awakening, has spent the past several years collecting a wealth of material pertaining to this great pole shift. A former research associate of astronaut Edgar Mitchell, the articulate magazine and book author believes that there is a good possibility the earth rotated at least once before, and is likely to do so once again sometime before the year 2000.

In order to get to the bottom of the matter, White has spent considerable time checking out the predictions of both select scientists and New Age seers who maintain that Terra Firma is in for a mighty jolt in the not so distant future.

"There are three main groups that independently predict a pole shift in this century," states White. "The first are the ancient prophecies spoken of in the Bible and by such soothsayers as Nostradamus. Edgar Cayce and Rev. Paul Solomon who maintain that on May 5, 2000, there will be a grand alignment of the planets which will induce shifting of the earth's crust. There is also Aaron Abrahams, a psychic in Washington State who says that in the year 1999 or 2000 the Earth will tumble on its axis a full 180 degrees, but the core of the earth will tumble only about 90 degrees so that the poles will in effect be projecting through the Equatorial regions. At this moment the present ice caps will build up in the polar locations. In addition to the ancient prophecies and the contemporary psychics, there are modern scientifically-oriented researchers who also claim that there is a pole shift coming."

Among the scientists White refers to are Hugh Auchincloss Brown, an electrical engineer who before his death at the age of 96, devoted more than 60 years of his life to the promulgation of his theory that a vast polar ice cap would tip the earth over toward the end of this century and wipe out civilization. Also, quoted by White in his book "Poleshift" (published by Doubleday) are the likes of Chan Thomas, a West Coast-based cosmologist, Charles Hapgood, a friend of Albert Einstein, and Adam Barber, an independent investigator who started his own foundation for advocates of the polar shift theory.

At a symposium which I organized in New York City, John White revealed the fact that his research has fully determined that a number of UFO contactees and channels have also been predicting a polar shift, as sort of a climax to earth changes that are getting under way now and will be continuing right on through to the end of this century.

What I find so fascinating about John White's work is that he looks at the potential outcome of a global disaster in a much different way than you might expect. He tries to see things in a positive light and says that we do have a chance to survive — that if we are destroyed we will have no one to blame but ourselves.

"Many of the predictions say that it will be the human factor — we ourselves — that will be of critical importance in either triggering or preventing these earth changes. In essence the psychics say that the state of our consciousness will determine the outcome of the approaching crisis."

John credits anthropologist and archaeologist, Dr. Jeffrey Goodman with devising a term to cover this human factor which will prove most important in determining our future state of affairs. "In the book *We Are the Earthquake Generation,*' Dr. Goodman uses the word 'Bio-relativity' to describe how human beings are effecting through the power of their thoughts everything that exists around them. Consciously or unconsciously our behavior has an influence on the totality of the earth. In this regard the prophecies tell us that virtuous living and respect for the earth can have a stabilizing impact. Prayer is a familiar form of this influence, but better yet would be the development of a steadily focused consciousness amongst the people that would recognize the mutual dependence of the human race and the cosmos, and the interdependence that we have on each other that really makes us the co-creators of our destiny."

John suggests that such a state of consciousness operating among the human race would have a strong, positive bearing on the future trials and tribulations. "The native Americans say we should 'walk in balance on the Earth Mother,' and if we don't the alternative is simple. If we continue our disregard for the sacredness of life, if we continue our crimes against nature and our fellow humans, the outcome could be bleak.

AN IMPORTANT CONVERSATION WITH JOHN WHITE

Around the time that his book *POLESHIFT* was published, I sat down with John and quizzed him extensively on a possible tilting of the Earth. This subject is certain to be of grave relevance to all of us. Here are some excerpts from our conversation:

Beckley: Looking to the future, if there were a polar shift in our lifetime, would that wipe out most of civilization?

White: My book *Poleshift* deals principally with the predictions and prophecies of another pole shift, a future one which is to occur by the end of this century — 1999 to 2000. A number of groups have independently predicted this. There are various ancient prophecies, notably those of the Bible, and the oracle Nostradamus, who say that the earth is probably going to tumble on its axis or shift its crust. They're not specific about the way this is going to happen.

Beckley: Specifically, what does the Bible say?

White: In Revelation it says that the earth will undergo an earthquake greater than has ever been recorded before, and by extension — since we do know that earthquakes do jolt the axis of the earth — this could produce a very traumatic pole shift.

Beckley: Is there evidence leading up to this?

White: In addition to the prophecies and the contemporary psychics, there are modern scientifically-oriented researchers who also claim that there is a pole shift coming. Immanuel Velakovsky, by the way did not predict another one. He simply dealt with the evidence of the previous ones. Another researcher is Professor Charles Hapgood who wrote a book called THE PATH OF THE POLES. Actually that was the title of the revised edition. The first edition was called EARTH'S SHIFTING CRUST. The introduction to that book was actually written by Albert Einstein, who endorsed Hapgood's notion. Of those who say another one is likely, nearly all of them agree that a pole shift will occur at the end of this century. But not all of them say that it is inevitable.

Beckley: Why do they say that it will happen at the end of this century?

White: That's a good question. I'm not really able to answer except to the extent that a number of factors have been identified by the various predictions and prophecies as being the trigger mechanisms or contributing some degree of influence to a forthcoming pole shift. These various factors — which are both internal to the earth and external, and natural as well as man made — are acting at different rates of speed and with different rates of influence. However, they are all converging at whatever their speed might be so as to come together at the end of this century, or thereabouts.

Beckley: You're talking now about the increase in earthquakes, volcanic eruptions, and so forth?

White: We are seeing evidence right now that the prophecies are being fulfilled. Clearly, the earth is coming out of a period in which it has been relatively free from earthquakes and volcanic activity, and is entering a time when seismic activity is stepping up. We are seeing more earthquakes, and more powerful earthquakes every year. We're seeing long-dormant volcanoes starting to erupt. There is one in Japan that erupted in October of 1979, and it has never been known in all of history to have erupted before.

This is a hotly debated topic, and by and large the scientific community does not accept it. But, I should say that on the other side of the question there is an informal study done by a friend of mine in Connecticut, who looked at the data available on four different volcanoes, two in the Caribbean and two in Italy. What he did was to plot the frequency of eruption for these volcanoes over the last 200 to 300 years. He found that these volcanoes, all four of them, are erupting more and more frequently. When he plotted out the eruption patterns for each of them, he discovered that all four converged in a 1982-1984 time period.

You asked what the effect of a pole shift would be. Within 24 hours, the results would be this: First of all the oceans would spill out of their basins and just overrun the land masses, in massive tidal waves. There would be huge earthquakes greater than we've ever measured. Volcanoes would erupt around the world. Poisonous gases and ash would fill the atmosphere. The earth itself would be tumbling through space at speeds of hundreds of miles an hour so in effect, anything living on the surface of the earth would experience hurricane winds of several hundred miles an hour. The face of the globe would change instantly. Not only climates, climatic zones, but land masses would rise and fall. Geography itself would change, and of course living organisms, including people, would be eliminated. There would be unprecedented destruction and death. Some predictions say that 90 percent or more of people on the earth would be killed in such a pole shift.

Beckley: Would we have any kind of luck in preventing such a global disaster?

White: This is a good example of how we can directly effect those predictions and prophecies. We can also do it through parapsychological means as well as overt behavior. We have seen recently the emergence of PK ability, or psychokinesis, especially in young children around the world. Hundreds of youngsters are developing

— 173 —

the ability to bend metal and influence matter using the power of their minds. Let's imagine that this trait emerges very quickly in the human race on a global scale. Conceivably if it were developed to a sufficient degree, in a large number of people, through the direct influence of mind over matter, we could pacify — we could stabilize — the earth even though it would be on the point of a pole shift. This is sort of science fantasy, but it's not totally incredible or beyond imagination.

Beckley: Granted, but would we have enough warning to so something like this?

White: The warning is in the predictions and prophecies. We have at most 20 years according to these predictions and prophecies. Now, I'm not saying this *is* going to happen. I'm saying that there is a serious case for a pole shift happening, and that the scientific community especially should examine it.

Beckley: Are you at all familiar with the fact that in UFO literature, the various UFO contactees who say they are having physical contact or telepathic contact with extraterrestrial beings are being told pretty much the same thing?

White: Yes, I am. In fact, I have a chapter in my book which covers one such prediction. It was made through Biard Wallace in Grosskill, Michigan, and the alleged communicants are the Space Brothers. The Space Brothers told Biard Wallace and his group that the whole solar system is moving into a new sector of space where the vibratory quality is going to be such as to change consciousness in the human race. At the same time, a new star will come into the solar system which will shift the center of gravity from its present location to another one as the solar system becomes a binary star solar system. The shift of the center of gravity will affect all the planets. Some will leave their orbits. Others will just get a shaking up in their orbits. But conceivably a pole shift could be devastating not only on earth but on other planets. And according to the Space Brothers, this will take place within the next 15 years.

Beckley: Are they going to try to do something to prevent this from happening?

White: I've not heard anything, or read anything in any communications about this. What they're trying to do, essentially, is awaken the human race to the possibility and encourage us to develop our own powers and abilities.

Beckley: Are they offering advice in this regard. Do you see this as an overall pattern in all of the experiences?

White: There is a pattern of sorts. By no means is there agreement from all the communications, from extraterrestrials and medaterrestrials. But generally speaking, the thrust of the communications is that a time of change is coming upon the earth.

On a more or less regular basis, John delves into such topics when he organizes a yearly UFO/New Age conference near his home. A schedule can be obtained by writing to White at Omega Communications, Box 2051, Cheshire, CT 06410.

On a positive note, John concludes by noting that there is a way out of the situation we are in.

"The predictions and prophecies all say that if we don't mend our ways we will have created a situation in which the planet is destabilized. The pole shift will result in destroying most life on our planet."

To a man, all of those we have sought knowledge from fully agree that even though these devastating events may occur, after the earth has settled down, a Golden Age will flourish for the first time since the days of Adam and Eve.

"The earth changes," states John White, "will never-the-less open up a niche in the environment for new life forms to emerge. The human race will be cleansed from the Earth Mother because it has become an irritating, infectious disease. But note that it will not be a case of our being punished for our sins. From the prospective of Bio-relativity it will be a case of being punished by our sins. It's instant Karma — getting back what we give. According to the prophecies there will be some survivors. These survivors will be the seedbed for a new race — a higher humanity — which will evolve in an accelerated fashion. The new race will know from first hand experiences what the terrible consequences are for failing to walk in balance upon the Earth Mother. The new race will know how to live in harmony with the cosmos and they will inherit the earth."

D-DAY SEERS SPEAK

To sum up and review these amazing psychic and UFO revelations, we call upon New Age teacher and master alchemist Michael X. Barton, author of many titilating monographs, to review the subject in the form of a series of questions which he asked of those who have first hand knowledge of the situation which is based on first hand visionary experiences.

Question: "Can you give me a clear word picture of D-DAY?"

Answer: "Yes. There are astrological signs foretelling that the Great Polar Shift will come soon. There will be great cataclysms and geological changes. The atomic blasts in the west have intensely aggravated the San Andreas Fault. It will crack wide open soon and great tremors will shake the state of California. . .and it will *gradually* submerge.

"At the time of the Shift there will be a terrific chain of earthquakes. Japan, two-thirds of the British Isles and the countries of the warring nations of Europe and the Balkans will be submerged. The Suez Canal will become an open waterway, due to the submergence of the land thereabout.

"New York City will be hit by a terrific earthquake and be submerged. Mountainous tidal waves will engulf the Atlantic coastline hundreds of miles inland. We will have a 50-foot flood level in Pittsburgh. Washington, D.C. will be flooded. The submerged islands of Atlantis will rise up in the Atlantic.

"A huge continent will rise up in the Pacific. The New Jerusalem will descend upon it. In the New Age (after the Great Polar Shift) you will be able to travel by water from the Gulf of Mexico to Hudson Bay; from Denver to Moscow. The Great Shift will come at the time of atomic warfare, which will be of short duration." — Brother Joseph A. Lageman, Pittsburgh, PA.

Question: "What places may be considered 'safety areas'?"

Answer: "We agree with the Mormons that the Rocky Mountain area is the best place in the world; that is, the area between the Sierra Nevada and Rocky Mountains. That takes in most of Colorado, the western part, the whole of Utah, most of Idaho and the northern part of Arizona. Montana and Wyoming should be good, for they have all the necessary factors for safety.

"That gives you plenty of scope. That doesn't mean to say that these are the only safe places. We believe the western part of Pennsylvania should be good, providing you are far enough away from the industrial cities, and have a good elevation. The minimum should be 2,000 feet. 4,000 would be better. And don't forget that the range of the atom bomb is much greater today than it was when tried in Japan.

"Keep away from large bodies of water, either oceans or lakes. Many lakes will spill their contents when the earth CHANGES ITS AXIS, which it is going to do. As far as the enemy is concerned, we believe certain cities will be immune from sabotage and warfare. But that does not exclude them from danger from the elements, such as earthquakes, cyclones, tornadoes, and tidal waves. And so, as the good Lord cleanses the earth, we must get out into the wide open spaces, and live close to nature. We shall be stripped of things that come from our artificial civilization, things that we do not need anyway. Not only will the land be cleansed, but HUMANITY WILL BE PURGED.

"Let me emphasize that all COASTAL REGIONS are dangerous, for there will be tidal waves such as have never prevailed in modern times, due to the sinking of large bodies of land and the rising of others. It is more likely that the islands of Japan will sink into the Pacific; and that close to the American coast will be the rising of a huge body of land, a portion if not the whole of ancient Lemuria. Tidal waves on the East Coast are apt to reach a height of from 1,000 to 2,000 feet. And so from that, you can see that the coastal regions are all dangerous." — Excerpt from "THE COMING STORM" by William Kullgren, Atascadero, California.

Question: "Is D-DAY inevitable, or can it be prevented?"

Answer: "No predicted event is entirely inevitable. Reverse forces, used in the present moment, can always minimize, lessen or prevent a future event from happening in the way it is likely to. According to Hugh Auchincloss Brown, E.E., we can postpone the impending flood. The suggested method is cutting many channels in the parapet of coastal rocks that form the basin which holds up the ·

great ice reservoir (at South Pole). This will prevent the central glacial ice to drain off into the oceans by gravity. We have a rendezvous with Fate. We will become our own corporeal saviors by taking control of and limiting the further growth of the South Polar Ice Cap, or most of our race will perish in the flood."

Question: "What will precede the Great Polar Shift?"

Answer: "Maybe a war. Economic result: poverty, then starvation. Be ready for great changes in the twinkling of an eye. Prepare for SEVEN YEARS of struggle with the elements." — Oxtle of Mars. Received by L. D. of Oxnard, Calif., 5-18-59.

Question: "Who shall be taken up by the Space People on D-DAY?"

Answer: "As your Holy Prophesy so states, we shall save the elect. We stand by with our craft of all types and sizes. We are constantly prepared to land if and when it should become necessary to evacuate the elect to new homes on nearby planets where they will be our guests until your planet has been completely washed and cleansed and made fit once more to dwell upon. . . ." Telethot communication received from Ashtar Command, Space Station Schare, by Carl A. Anderson, of Fullerton, California.

"Thousands will be rescued from off the land surfaces just prior to the cataclysmic upheavals. They will be levitated or lifted up, and taken aboard the craft you have chosen to call 'Flying Saucers' . . . There will be many who will not be taken up, who will be spared however. They will be in places of comparative safety when disaster strikes. They will be saved by the protective force-field emanating from the aura that surrounds their bodies. . . ." — Message received by Automatic Writing by Carl A. Anderson on February 25, 1957, from a Master now in Tibet.

Question: "Shall we build boats or rafts for survival?"

Answer: "The masses will need them. Those whose aura radiates much light, with an abundance of the violet or purple tone will *not* need them. They shall be taken up. Your greatest protection lies in building your aura — filling it with more and more LIGHT — and cleansing it, day by day. The best way to expand and strengthen your aura with the light will be revealed to you very soon. Be alert to accept and apply this vital new information." — Lon-Zara received by Michael X.

"On August 26, 1958, a dear friend of mine, Wanda Brown and one of her friends, of Inglewood, California, were advised by Blaru (a being from another solar system) that the best kind of boat to build was 'circular and covered with a hatch. Food supplies sufficient for several months at sea should be taken.' I agree that the 'saucer-shaped' boat or raft is far superior to the ordinary kind. However, we are now being requested by our nearest planetary guardians to concentrate on building our spiritual aura rather than on building of the rafts." — Michael X.

Question: "What is happening to our Solar System now?"

Answer: "Several years ago our Solar System passed into a new phase called the '4th Density'. This new phase is now changing our entire earth and our way of life. Prior to this time everything as we know it consisted of three Densities: Life, Motion, and Consciousness. Now a new and higher level of Life is going to occur. (The Spiritual or Christ Consciousness.) Every individual person whose (soul) education has been complete must PREPARE for this, this next step of our eternal existence. Those not ready must take this step over again. Our planet, entering this new Density, shall endure changes that will eventually be CATACLYSMIC in action.

"After the readjustment of our planet, a new way of life will begin. The people will enjoy the pleasure of space travel; there will be no disease nor sickness, hence no need for doctors or for hospitals. Everyone will communicate with each other through thought transference; the need for speech will not be. Wars, hatred and lust for power will be unheard of. Everyone will be on equal level. The Way of Life will be as the Creator intended it to be. Love, Peace and Harmony will reign supreme." — Telethot received by Russell Dunham of Fullerton, Calif.

Question: "What is my responsibility in these turbulent times?"

Answer: "New adventures, new lands, new friends — seek ye out those who are in accord. Be in rapport with those who are bearers of LIGHT. Seek ye the Ambassadors from out the Cosmic Realms. Many are the Ambassadors now come to GUIDE the race of man into pathways of light, lest man fall into the pit of destruction. Be thou aware of these Beings who are ever watchful of thy purpose.

"Open thy consciousness to their messages. Listen intently for their instruction. Ask that these shall be aware of thy cosmic contact DURING THE HOURS OF SLEEP. Pray thou will be cognizant of thy nightly experiences.

"Receptivity is for thy experience. Calm thyself and listen for the 'wee small voice'. Amplify this voice with thy enthusiasm and broadcast it to the four corners of the Earth. BE THY VOICE!" — Larry Dodge of Oxnard, Calif. Telethot 8-22-56.

Michael concludes his findings with these closing words. "Again, dear friend, the Wise Ones of both ancient and modern times have spoken to us. They have spoken of D-DAY and what it will mean to you and me. Their words only serve to bring us closer in the bond of universal LOVE and UNDERSTANDING that exists between every living thing.

"It is important that you may share your love and light with others, wisely, but with NEW ZEAL. For you — a NEW AGE Individual — have heard the CLARION CALL OF THE SEERS. And you have a place, a service, an opportunity to help bring in the glorious Millennium and GOD'S KINGDOM ON EARTH!"

A LESSON TO BE LEARNED

As we are about to close this book of revelations, perhaps our outlook on life and our feelings toward our world and the people who we must share this space with, have changed. When you take into consideration all the events that are slated to happen, you can see that it doesn't matter one single bit what your political views are, what church you go to (if any), or how much money you have in the bank. We are all traveling through space at the same speed and toward an identical destiny. Rich or poor, famous or unknown, handsome or ordinary looking, these are definitely not the questions of importance which face us in the Last Days. When the earth tremors start and the volcanoes erupt we are all equal beings circling the sun.

If there is consolation in any of this it must be in the knowledge that we — the New Agers of the world — have a jump on the rest of

John White's book POLE SHIFT examines the prospects of a cataclysmic shifting of the North and South Poles before the end of the century. The results of such an event are huge tidal waves, volcanic eruptions, devastating hurricane winds, and earthquakes.

humanity. We have sought the "Light of Understanding" and have grown from that which we have been shown. Many of us have felt the hand of an unseen force during the course of our lives. We know that we are not the only intelligent creatures in the universe, and we know that beings from other realms have been here since the dawn of time to assist us in climbing the ladder to higher vibrations. We realize quite fully that earth is but a stepping stone for us, a schoolhouse where we have been sent to learn a lesson. If we are able to deal with life and death we have nothing to fear, even if it should be too late to stop the impending catastrophies. We know that our existence is eternal, that our spirit lives on, and that it is up to us and *not* fate that determines our true future.

Dear Reader:

Before you put this book aside, please turn the page and take part in a special meditation which has come to us direct from the Ashtar Command. This message was beamed to earth for the express purpose of providing a personal sense of peace, harmony, love and prosperity in each of our lives.

Behold the New Age is before us!

Love & Light
Tim Beckley

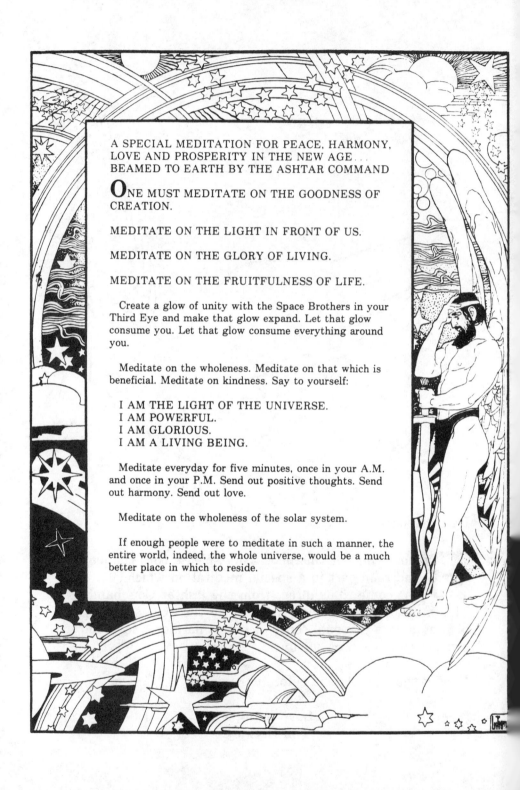

A SPECIAL MEDITATION FOR PEACE, HARMONY, LOVE AND PROSPERITY IN THE NEW AGE... BEAMED TO EARTH BY THE ASHTAR COMMAND

ONE MUST MEDITATE ON THE GOODNESS OF CREATION.

MEDITATE ON THE LIGHT IN FRONT OF US.

MEDITATE ON THE GLORY OF LIVING.

MEDITATE ON THE FRUITFULNESS OF LIFE.

Create a glow of unity with the Space Brothers in your Third Eye and make that glow expand. Let that glow consume you. Let that glow consume everything around you.

Meditate on the wholeness. Meditate on that which is beneficial. Meditate on kindness. Say to yourself:

I AM THE LIGHT OF THE UNIVERSE.
I AM POWERFUL.
I AM GLORIOUS.
I AM A LIVING BEING.

Meditate everyday for five minutes, once in your A.M. and once in your P.M. Send out positive thoughts. Send out harmony. Send out love.

Meditate on the wholeness of the solar system.

If enough people were to meditate in such a manner, the entire world, indeed, the whole universe, would be a much better place in which to reside.

RECOMMENDED SOURCES FOR ADDITIONAL INFORMATION

INNER LIGHT MAGAZINE
Box 753, New Brunswick, NJ 08903
(Edited by the author, Timothy G. Beckley)

MARK-AGE INFORM-NATIONS
Box 2900368, Ft. Lauderdale, FL 33329

UFO UNIVERSE
531 W. 54th St., New York, NY 10019
(Only UFO newsstand magazine published in U.S.)

STELLAR RESEARCH INSTITUTE
Box 74, Kempton, IL 60946

DR. FRANK E. STRANGES
Box 5, Van Nuys, CA 91401

DELVAL UFO
948 Almshouse Rd., Ivyland, PA 18794
(Channels Lynn & Anthony Volpe)

BLUE ROSE MINISTRY
Box 332, Cornville, AZ 86325
(Channel, Robert Short)

GUARDIAN ACTION INTERNATIONAL
Box 27725, Salt Lake City, UT 84127
(Channel, Thelma Terrell/Tuella)

A.S.S.K.
Box 35, Mt. Shasta, CA 96076
(Channel, Sister Thedra)

WILDFIRE
Box 148, Tum Tum, WA 99034
(Publication of Sun Bear)

SHAMAN'S DRUM
Box 16507, North Hollywood, CA 91615
(Contains Indian Prophecies)

ABOUT THE AUTHOR

In 1957 Timothy Green Beckley experienced his first of four UFO sightings. Almost immediately he became intrigued with the subject and ever since has traveled extensively to gather facts and information about this global phenomenon. Several years ago he was invited to speak before a special committee in England's House of Lords where he addressed members of Parliament on the "Cosmic Watergate."

During the late 1960s, Beckley founded one of the first New Age centers. The New York School of Occult Arts and Sciences became the springboard for many of today's most respected parapsychologists, psychics and metaphysical teachers.

Engaging in diverse activities, over the years Beckley has been a successful movie maker, a producer of rock music, and author of numerous books including, *KAHUNA POWER, MJ-12 & THE RIDDLE OF HANGAR 18, BOOK OF SPACE*

BROTHERS, PEOPLE OF THE PLANET CLARION, THE SHAVER MYSTERY & THE INNER EARTH, ROCK RAPS OF THE 70s, PROPHECY OF THE PRESIDENTS, STRANGE ENCOUNTERS, just to name a few.

During the years when few dared talk about UFOs and alien beings, Beckley appeared on radio and TV talk shows helping to keep the subject "alive." His widely distributed journals INNER LIGHT and UFO REVIEW go to readers in 17 countries with a combined circulation of over one hundred thousand. Just recently, he was selected to edit *UFO UNIVERSE,* the first slick UFO publication to be sold on newsstands nationally. He is also president of *Inner Light Publications* a publishing firm which specializes in books on New Age subjects by such highly respected authorities as Brad Steiger, John Keel and T. Lobsang Rampa. As author of this book, he has made an extensive study of prophecy from Nostradamus to the most recent forecasts which involve many startling revelations.

The author, Timothy Green Beckley, stands in front of Stonehenge during a recent world tour.

FREE CATALOG